THE BOOK OF PROMISE

CONVERSATIONS WITH RAFAEL

ON HEALING HUMANITY NOW

ELS VAN POPPEL M.A.

1

Published by Wild Wings Productions: Ferny Way, Ferny Hills 4055, Queensland, Australia.

Cover Photography: Cairo Sauvage
Cover Design: Els van Poppel and Cairo Sauvage

https://elsvanpoppel.com

The information in this book is not to be treated as a substitute for professional medical advice – always consult a medical practitioner. Any use of information in this book is at the reader's discretion and risk. It is not a replacement for medical or mental health care given by physicians or trained medical personnel. The author is not to be held responsible for any loss, claim or damage arising out of the use, or misuse, of suggestions made, the failure to take medical advice or for any material on third party websites. By continuing to view this book, readers indicate acceptance of these terms. Readers who do not accept these terms should not access, use, interact with or view this book.

"There is no wrathful God. There is no God who requires violence or oppression, murder or intimidation to make His point or keep humanity 'in line'. There is no God who encourages anyone to hate, bully, discriminate, torture, murder, or rape. There is no God who would spur anyone into being brutal, or slaughter the very own people She created and loves. God, the Divine Source of all, is one of unconditional love, no matter how you manifest as a human being in life: as to who you are, as to where you're from, as to what the color of skin is, as to what sex or sexual orientation you may be. Rich or poor, you are all created in the image of the Divine. You are all equal. You are unique expressions of the Creator and you are all part of His Great Love, of Her Great Love. As such, you are all unconditionally loved and respected. No individual or group should ever be persecuted in the name of God. Rather, each individual, each group, is to be loved, celebrated and respected for their own uniqueness and manifestation. Because it is through their uniqueness that each individual contributes to the rich tapestry of life."

Raphael 2018

"Although it tackles some weighty subject matter, it is just so easy and pleasurable to read. The Book of Promise addresses many of the concern and big questions that we all have. It acknowledges the huge challenges we face, both individually and on a larger scale, and offers a feeling of being empowered to help yourself and humanity to make the world a wonderful and healthy place for all of us.

It's like a warm comforting hug for the mind, heart and spirit."

Vicki Englund – writer, screenwriter, arts reviewer

TABLE OF CONTENTS

PART 2 – HEALING HUMANITY   99

A NOTE FROM THE AUTHOR

I was born in the South of the Netherlands and was raised amongst a vast, extended family.

One night, at the age of four, I experienced a vivid apparition. A large and light-filled angelic being appeared in the top corner of my room, lighting up the whole room. The apparition was very real and I was very frightened, so I fled to my parents' bedroom. My level-headed father convinced me that I had probably had a dream, and not to worry about it. However, I knew what I had seen. I knew what was floating above my wardrobe so I stayed in my parents' room for many weeks to come until the intensity of the angelic experience slowly started to fade. From then on, I became good at closing off from anything that 'hovered' around the edges of earthly reality, and just to be sure I kept a light on in my room for years.

I emigrated from the Netherlands to Australia, and at the age of 30, my world came crushing down when my dear beloved oldest brother suddenly died in a car accident. Ripped from his young life through no fault of his own, he left behind a loving wife and three young children under the age of four.

I was stunned and in total disbelief. The sudden realization that life could end in one split second really hit home – and that it could happen to my strong brother, who really had his life together and was invincible in my eyes. It totally rocked my belief system. I went through the motions of profound grief and knew that life was never going to be the same. It set me on my quest to get closer to an understanding of the meaning of life.

At times, I thought back to the apparition during my childhood. I had always felt that I was protected in life by an unseen 'entity', a protective being who always had my very best interests at heart. I would call upon my guide to assist me – to sit on the bonnet of my car during bad weather, to protect me if I had to walk along a dark road at night, to help me get through a job interview – and I did receive the support if I asked for it. Still, I was scared to open up to this presence.

I went on to lecture at a university. Even though I loved working with the students, I was a little frustrated. I felt that what they needed most was some guidance in life matters. Unfortunately, I couldn't offer this within the confinement of the syllabus. At the same time my guest for meaning kept increasing and I wasn't finding the answers I longed for. I knew I was avoiding to pay attention to the entity that had always stood beside me.

So one day, I realized I had to overcome my fear of the childhood visitation and allow the door to communication to open up. I sent a clear message 'out there' that I probably couldn't deal with another frightening apparition but that I was eager to listen. I kept a notebook and a pen ready and asked the questions: Was there a way in which I could be of service, for the highest good of all, maybe on a larger scale? If so, was my protector available for some guidance?

It is quite astounding when you 'hear' a sentence that is not reaching you through auditory perception, saying, "Yes, there is". When you are given a sentence that is reaching you without thought, saying, "I am Raphael. I am here to assist you, dear beloved soul."

Although his being felt very familiar, I still had hesitations about allowing his ethereal presence into my life. I had been so used to closing of from the celestial energy for so long that the whole idea of finally opening up was still filling me with uncertainty and doubt. Did I really want to put myself in this vulnerable position and continue this journey into the unknown?

I had been writing down his communications for some weeks, and although I had trusted his words due to the goodness they expressed, I kept asking for confirmation that the communications were indeed coming from the highest and purest place. That he was indeed Raphael, the angelic guide. I went through the motions of asking sign after sign, and remarkably he always 'obliged' so much so that I started to feel rather silly for requesting constant confirmations. How many of these 'signs' did I need? How much energy was I prepared to waste, when deep down I knew the truth of who he was... when I knew the direction my life was about to take? I decided to stop questioning the obvious and embrace his presence and the task at hand.

I kept scribbling down the sentences in my notebook and allowed the communication to flow freely, without questioning, without thinking. It was only after a few months that I started reading back the writings and putting them into digital format. It was then that I was taken by the profoundness of the messages. It was as if Raphael was directly answering some of the questions I had had for a long time. It was as if he was addressing my angsts about life and the current concerns for humanity and the state of our planet. I was surprised about his message of urgent sustainability measures, especially because I hadn't paid enough attention to that aspect in life myself. I felt quite ashamed that I hadn't taken more renewable action, and went on to order solar panels for our house immediately.

Even though I have stayed true to Raphael's 'tone of voice' and the messages he has given, there have been instances where the text was quite 'dense' and complex in its wording. Therefore, I had to slightly reword some of the paragraphs to make the text more readable for a wider audience, without changing the truth and essence of his message.

I would never have thought that I would ever write about the Divine Consciousness. And by no means do I, as a person, profess to be all-knowing in the mystery of life or being able to provide all answers with regards to the Divine Creation. However, I am grateful for having been able to pass on Raphael's words and I can now see how they make sense in the ongoing turmoil that is currently threatening our lives. I have accepted that Raphael, as he mentions, is "trusting our working relationship" and I'm happy to spread his message of healing and love.

FEBRUARY- RAPHAEL

I am Raphael, I am here to assist you, dear beloved soul.

I have observed your struggles in the last few decades. Your journey has not always been an easy one, however it has been the path you have manifested and which you were meant to travel.

You are a shiny light to many others yet spirit needs your time now to focus on the task that you were meant to perform all along. Due to your life experiences and your sensitivities and skills, you will aid in the writing of what will be known as 'The Book of Promise'.

The 'Book of Promise' will be centered on your current need for global healing. Healing on an individual level as much as the healing of humanity and the magnificent planet you all inhabit. I will shine a light on the much needed work in the support and creation of self-love. In the much needed task of aligning yourselves with your soul purpose: of contributing to an increased thriving humanity, a healthier planet earth and an all-encompassing love for all.

You live in a time of transformation and many souls have incarnated to witness the change in spiritual paradigm. Please bear with me. I know you are taking your task seriously and I acknowledge you for that. I know you are overcome with questions but please trust the process of our working relationship.

I have witnessed your questioning of my appearance and my being. You have tested my presence over and over again, needing confirmation that I truly am Raphael, your angelic guide, and why it is indeed me, who is appearing to you.

As you may or may not be aware, I have been known to assist many souls during times of healing, and in your present time, your planet and all of humanity are in desperate need of revitalization. It is sadly true that your magnificent planet, its glorious creation, is now in a state of malady, and humanity as you know it, is in serious danger of extinction.

THE CURRENT MALADY

Times of much needed transformation are upon you. The malady we have sadly observed from the angelic realm may be recognizable for you all.

Your lives have been determined by the rapid advancement of technology, parts of which have overstepped their welcome, defying the purpose of the initial intention, which was to serve humanity rather than provide opportunities to destroy it.

Often, faith is missing from your modern day life and instead we, in the angelic realm, sadly perceive more fear. Fear of aloneness. Fear of failing. Fear of missing out. Fear of the other. Fear of war and loss.

Your essential human need for love, support, companionship and a sense of belonging, is not always sufficiently being met. Instead we witness increasing levels of loneliness, a growth in substance abuse and a rapidly rising disconnect from those who matter most, including your families and children. Community living is almost becoming a sad obsolescence; instead we observe a growth in human separation and isolation.

States of anxious and stressful living and exhaustion and a lack of meaning, or life purpose, have been detected amongst many of you. The coping mechanisms of addictions as well as the desire for vast consumerism, are no cure for this sense of purposeless existence. On the contrary, these mechanisms of grappling with reality only enhance the state of disconnect, and bring one further from the truth: a state of happiness, joy and meaning.

Please do not despair, and bear with me as I continue briefly.

The shift away from the authentic self has been replaced by a growth in ego adoration, spreading via your devices, disconnecting the individual from the other, as much as from the true self and your Divine sense of being.

The state of disconnect causes excessive reactions within your societies in that acts of violence and terror are occurring more frequently and therefore the true bond of humanity is being tarnished. Rather than viewing the stranger through the eyes of the inherent good and love in all, the overwhelming emotions of doubt, wariness, anger and suspicion take over.

Mass production of life-destroying weapons and artillery is sadly being fueled by expansive levels of greed. This sorrowful worldwide conduct is being justified and marketed by leaders, through a rhetoric of fear-based thoughts, actions and reactions – a self-feeding industry of greed, fear, destruction and pain.

Please bear with, my observation of the current malady is nearly finished. My tone will change. I will help you with answers.

On a primary level, your wholesome and nutritious foods have been transformed through mass manufacturing and processing, therefore having lost many of their crucial and essential nutrients. Instead, addictive and harmful components are being added, causing lingering ailments and disease. The purposeful manipulation and contamination of your precious foods is once again driven by desires for endless profits, all this to the detriment of humanity's wellbeing.

And this, dear beloved, is taking place, while the beautiful creation of your majestic home, the Divine creation of your planet earth, is being exhausted. Mass production resulting in vast amounts of suffocating waste and lethal products are threatening all that is: your habitable environments, your airways, your waterways, your co-creations of fauna and flora, your fellow human beings, your chance of joyful living, your livelihoods, your very sense of being. You.

For all of this, my dear beloved, the time has come for me to come your way. The time has come for you to be reminded of who you really are. Of why you are actually here. Of living your life on purpose. Your true purpose. And how you can heal – yourselves, each other and the majestic planet you inhabit.

I am here to bring you awareness and to remind you all of your individual strength, your inner power, that has been given to you and is with you all. I am here to guide you to a knowing that change is possible, that your humanity can thrive, that happiness can be achieved and that your planet can be healthy again. I am here to remind you of the tools and the assistance that are at hand, unconditionally, and for all. At any time, any place, anywhere... as you so desire or will upon.

And it is for this purpose, dear beloved, that I wholeheartedly welcome you. I welcome you to my sincere word of healing. I welcome you to a testimonial of hope, created in the context of your current time as you know it. I welcome you with all my heart, with all my love. And with that, I welcome you, profoundly and unconditionally loving, to my word, in assistance of all of humanity, in all of creation. I welcome you to:

'The Book of Promise'
Conversations with Rafael.

WHAT IS NEW?

Elements of spiritual wisdom have been conveyed and repeated over thousands of years and one may ask: "What is new, Raphael? Why you? Why now?"

Yes, indeed, many elements of spiritual wisdom have been forwarded and practiced over thousands of years, and even though my messages are unique in their timing and the presentation of content, there are also some elements that have been brought to the awareness of humanity many times before. The important difference at this very moment in time is the imminence of the message as contained within these writings. Even though these words need not necessarily be considered a doomsday warning, there is a pressing need for the acceleration of spiritual awareness and an expansion of love amongst all human beings, and the application of it in your day-to-day lives. This is in order to save yourselves, to save humanity and the beautiful planet you inhabit.

From the angelic realm, it has been observed that currently, much of your spiritual practices occur within the confined walls of your churches, your mosques, your synagogues and your temples. I will refer to this as confined spiritual practice.

Even though confined spiritual practices serve an important purpose, the reality is that expansive spiritual growth amongst humanity is currently not being achieved within the restricted time and space of the confined religious activity. On the contrary, the sad observation has been that once the Divine intention has been set, within the confined walls of your houses of God, the doors to the world open and the floodgates of the ego-driven activities open up. The virtues of the Divine are then immediately set aside for greed-driven activities that benefit the individual, often at the expense of others and the planet you inhabit. Actions of harm and disservice to others are being justified under the term of 'progress' and for the ego-driven benefit of some. The full implementation of Divine virtues, within the arcs of your lives, is therefore incomplete, stagnating the spiritual awareness and understanding within humanity.

The moment is now for each and every one of you to realize the full potential of living your lives on purpose – of implementing the virtues of the Divine within the plenitudes of your lives, with confidence and knowing that one is protected. The time has come to bring down the walls of distrust, of anger and fear – to include joyful living and the virtues of love, kindness, compassion, wisdom, non-judgment, patience, and respect into the completeness of your day-to-day lives.

The need for humanity to step up is now. The call to living the principles of the Divine Truth is made with urgency and imminence. Each change within the individual will be multifold and have flow-on effects on humanity, expansively and immediately. And I am here to give you the tools, within the context of your contemporary lives. I am here to help you find the confidence and the faith – that you can make changes; that you can live a peaceful and happy life and that humanity can thrive.

I am here to remind you of who you really are. I am here to urge you to contain your anger, to swallow your pride, to set aside differences and to love the other like one should love oneself. Not just within the walls of the confined spiritual practice but in the totality of your day-to-day lives, with complete love towards yourselves and towards others, in the vast reality of the now and in the entirety of your lives on earth.

I am here to make you aware that you can find purpose in your earthly incarnation, that your existence is crucial and of the utmost importance... that your individual contribution is of the highest good. Now is the time to remember that humanity's true 'salvation lies within'. In this context, I am not speaking of salvation in relation to sin, rather salvation in the logical context of preservation from harm, ruin or loss. Humanity needs to survive and the capacity for its saving lies within each and every one of you. In aligning your actions with the wisdom of the Divine guidance within, and subsequently following the true purpose of your soul, your individual contribution will have more impact and exponential effect than what most of you are currently aware of. Through the practice of daily meditation, or prayer, the Divine knowledge and wisdom stemming from the shared consciousness can be accessed, and now is the time to reshape humanity's fate through your individual soul support.

PART 1 – HEALING 'THE SELF'

THE GREATEST LOVE OF ALL

As a humanity, you are all created in the image of the Great Divine Love, of Spirit, of God. Therefore, you are all part of this Great Intelligence, this infinite field of opportunities and creation, where all inspiration comes from, where all imagination lies. The Divine Consciousness, from which you were all born and to which you shall return, upon leaving your earthly incarnation, once your unique and physical life purpose has been fulfilled.

As you are all part of this infinite field of intelligence and Divine opportunity and Source, you are all connected and you are all, essentially, one. As such, you have access to this realm of opportunities, to this sphere of unconditional support. As part of the Divine Consciousness, it is your birthright to experience a beautiful, joyful and loving manifestation of your life – a life lived on a healthy planet, on purpose and with meaning, as part of a humanity that is thriving.

So it is that deep within your souls exists the greatest love of all. Unlike the romantic love, this love is accessible for each and every one of you at any moment in your lives, at any place, at any time, anywhere. To put it simply, you are loved unconditionally and vastly, beyond the constrictions of time, dimension or place, and beyond any possible human imagination.

You are vastly loved, right now – in this very moment in time. No matter what your current situation is, no matter how much others judge or condemn you. No matter how much your ego may dislike you, or feel shame. You are loved, in and beyond your physical manifestation, deeply and mightily.

The great miraculous 'you' is right here and you are endlessly supported. It is part of the purpose of your lives to reconnect with the Divine within, and become aware of its vast potential to create, and the unconditional love and support it has on offer. It is part of your life's journey to be inspired by this boundless meadow of potential, to connect to it and to create your lives accordingly – like walking through a field with many different flowers, each with their own color, shape, scent and size. To create your unique bouquet of life, grand and majestic, like no other one has ever been created. Like a piece of music, with its exclusive selection of notes, its very own composition, its selection of instruments, its particular rhythm, beating to its own unique beat.

It's your journey to recognize the voice of the Divine, to observe it, to listen to it, to embrace its wisdom, to feel its guidance, and to act from it, with confidence. It is your journey to rediscover this guiding voice within. To know that you can truly rely on it and that you are eternally supported by it.

Accessing the intelligence, love and support of the all-encompassing love can be through daily moments of stillness, meditation or inner prayer. In these sacred moments of meditation, the chatter of the brain is silenced and the inner wisdom can be sensed – like a quiet inner voice, a sense of knowing, nudging you in the right direction. Daily meditation enhances the skill of understanding the inner whispers of the Divine and how to gain inspiration and support from its instructions and directions.

The inner compass, the essence of your being, will always guide you from your heart. And as per manifestation design, your logic will strengthen the physical path you are meant to manifest and follow, but it is your heart that knows the way. It is your heart that knows your life's purpose and the unique manner in which you will contribute to a betterment of humanity at large. Once you have aligned yourself with the true path of your heart, with the calling of your soul, your brain will assist in the execution of the day-to-day practicalities, to support your unique physical manifestation, as you travel the path of life. The need to align yourselves with the direction of the Divine, the compass during your travels, is now greater than ever. The urgency to manifest a better, happier and healthier life for each individual, for each group, for each culture, and for humanity at large, is real. The time has arrived, the call is being made, to heal each individual, to heal all life on earth, and the moment to do it, is right here, right now.

As each individual reconnects to the intelligence of the shared consciousness within, the effects on humanity will be multifold and vast. The vibrational level of life will be raised, and love, compassion and understanding will be spread, throughout humanity, throughout the world.

In order to put this shift in awareness into the wider context of creation, I need to take a step back and refer to the beginning of time.

If the next chapter proves too abstract for you, I suggest you continue with the chapter, LOVE OF SELF

THE BEGINNING OF CREATION AND YOUR SOUL'S PURPOSE

In the beginning, there was just one, the infinite intelligence of the Creator, the all-encompassing loving and Divine Source of all, the One Great Love, the Divine Consciousness. The infinite intelligence, its purity, like a gentle song, floating through the skies of eternity, constituting eternal life.

The creation of the earth, with all its inhabitants, its flora and its fauna was the design of Divine Source. The highest vibration of loving light. Of God, who is omnipresence and in your understanding can be considered both male and female, both Ying and Yang, both fire and water, both earth and wind, both contracting and expanding within the eternal realms of loving awareness.

The purpose of the earthly creation was to manifest the ideas of the all-encompassing love into a physical expression, whereby non-physical consciousness was able to come into being and create in a sphere that contained substance and personification. In simple words, the Creator manifested the grand idea, the detail of all involved. From atoms, to molecules, to magnetic fields, physical beings were created from the omnipresent and infinite intelligence. Every organism, every flower, every insect, was created from Divine

Consciousness and in human terms, 'God made it work' – the precious beats of your hearts, the delicate functions of your organs, the growth of your hairs, the sensitivities of your skins. The beloved creation of all is one of extreme intelligence and consists of a delicate balance where every detail is designed according to the highest and most loving, creative order.

As you were created in this Divine image, you are part of the Divine Source, of the Great Intelligence, of Eternal Life, and as such, your earthly experience is in fact the experience of Divine Source. Even though Divine Source has all the intelligence about life and knowledge of truth, He can only experience the physical manifestation of His intelligence, in each and every earthly situation, through you. As such, you are a vehicle to Her experience and a medium of Her creation. God is within you. You are part of God. "I am" is to be considered the personification of the Divine Consciousness, in the physical existence. You are part of *all that is*.

31

Therefore, access to the power to create, in line with the Divine, is with and within you.

The physical expression however, has brought along limitations of substance and dimension. Hence, your earthly existence only knows three dimensions, which currently inhibits your complete understanding of eternal life and truth. Do not despair however and continue to read.

The precise and spectacular mechanism of the actual brain was created to hold the (limited) intelligence regarding the existence in the physical sphere, and to steer the body of the individual as needed through its physical journey on earth. As indicated, the brain is a fine and powerful mechanism, which processes some of the vast intelligence as needed for the manifestation of life in the three-dimensional physical world. As such, it filters vast amounts of Divine intelligence, processing the information needed to support the creation and survival of the physical existence. As part of the solid expression, the concept of the individual personality, or ego, was created, and in turn the personality was governed by the workings of the human brain. Through the manifestation of the individual (organisms), the illusion of separateness (from Divine Consciousness) was conceived. Yet it is only the limited three-dimensional understanding of the human brain that feeds the idea of separateness.

In reality however, your connection to the Divine and its vast intelligence are still with you, right here. As the navel in the physical body can be considered the remnants of the umbilical cord to the mother, so are the crucial links to the Divine Consciousness still housing within your physical body. Manifesting as actual cells of intelligence, this cluster of neurons, this connection to the Divine, this communication center of the heart, the link to eternal life, is located in the center of your chest. From this location, this umbilical cord to the Divine operates as a quiet voice within. It pulsates outwards and nudges you along, alerting you at times, as it helps to steer the direction of your physical manifestation, according to its purpose, along your path of life.

Over many lifetimes, communication between the heart center and the brain has always been of crucial importance. Your ancient cultures understood the importance of the whispers of the heart and the intuitive sense of knowing it brought along. It warned of approaching danger and made long-distance communications within the tribe possible. Nudges from the heart instructed the actions of the brain, and due to its importance, the Divine voice was celebrated, practiced and honored on a daily basis. A sense of spiritual belonging and protection made the path of life more fluent and peaceful to travel.

As technology advanced your modern-day cultures, the false belief that the human brain could steer your complete lives took over. Spiritual practices diminished in favor of ego- driven external purpose and entertainment of life. As less and less attention was paid to the voice of the Divine, the actual cells of intelligence, of the heart center, were underutilized within your physical manifestation, and as such your heart centers, as beacons of your Divine guidance and light, have started to shrink within your physical bodies.

As a consequence of these unfortunate developments, your lives have become more difficult to navigate than many lifetimes ago. Your outer accomplishments bring you ease, yet your sense of purpose and belonging have been diminished, leaving you empty and lost. The compass to your lives is now working less efficiently, leaving you to wander through life, searching for a sense of purpose.

Hence the time has arrived for me to remind you, as to who you are – to remind you of your connection to Source and to remind you of the reason as to why you are here. I am here to help you heal, to help you reconnect with your true purpose... so you can be in awe and embrace the very gift of life, and so you can live in line with the consciousness of the Divine, to find and experience love, for self and humanity at large. I am here to remind you to call upon the

Divine support. To emphasize the importance of repeated spiritual practice, so your heart centers will be strengthened, in accordance with your greater path – in line with your grander purpose, as you reconnect to the whispers from within. So it can help you on your journey – a path of following true purpose rather than wallowing in meaninglessness. A path of soul reward rather than missed opportunities and feelings of emptiness. I'm here to remind you of the importance of the connection to the loving voice within. Through meditation, through prayer. Through paying inward attention, through requesting help, and through listening. Daily, whether in nature, whether in churches, whether in temples, whether in your homes.

As one starts to recognize the inner guidance, one realizes that it differs profoundly from the voice of the ego in that it doesn't reason with you. It doesn't argue, it doesn't pressure; rather it soothes. Hate, anger, despair, irritation, dissatisfaction and disgust are expressions that can only be directed by the ego. Love, kindness, compassion, forgiveness and joy are expressions directed by the Divine voice: as it comes from the quiet unattached perspective, looking from above, down at your physical life, noticing you in the middle of your circumstances, showing the wider point of view and context.

It communicates, through your inner sense, what is right and what is wrong and it leaves you with a sense of knowing, as to what to do and what not to do. It informs you what feels 'right' and what feels 'wrong'. This inner voice, this guidance from your heart, from the consciousness within, is your all-encompassing guiding light to life.

With repeated practice, a true direction on the path of life can be taken – a direction that feels right, in accordance with your authentic desires and in honor of your true purpose. So you can make your unique contributions, so you can assist life on earth. So you can live your life in line with the true destiny of your soul.

And as your awareness grows, an overwhelming sense of protection, joy, and being deserving of love, will encompass you – a strong knowing that the inner Divine, the essence of who you are, has your back. That it supports you, and that you can trust it, with confidence and joy. It won't argue with you, it won't judge. It will direct you, from the highest good, for the right way forward, for you, for your fellow human beings, in your earthly life, in your physical manifestation.

Even if the results don't appear immediately, the actual workings (behind the scenes) will have been set in motion. You may be asked to have patience, or bite your tongue, or wait for better times, but the Divine force does know your true path once the right intention has been set. It will guide you to the manifestation of your highest good – safely and lovingly. Your inner guidance, the connection to the Divine Consciousness, the authentic 'you', the greatest love of all, is available to you, right here, right now...

As 'time' is a concept relating to the physical three-dimensional existence, rather than the infinite realm, the earthly creation is to be considered as still evolving. And in that context, you are still evolving.

It is part of the spiritual journey of each individual soul, to find its way back to the vast truth of the all-loving consciousness, and apply the workings of the Divine in the physical sphere so that the perfection of God's creation can be manifested in its completeness and all its truth. As such, it is your calling and your soul purpose to look after the wellbeing of yourselves as well as each other, and to maximize your potential for happiness and joy within the framework of your physical lives and the circumstances of your existence.

The first and most crucial step is the creation of a true love of self.

LOVE OF SELF

To be aware that you are born from true love and therefore authentically deserving of love is your birthright. Allowing the Divine Love into your life, and reconnecting to its powerful guidance and support, lies with and within you. The spiritual healing of you lies within you. Watch the thoughts of criticism that your limited ego and 'thinking brain' bring upon you.

As discussed, the ego has protected your physical manifestation, lifetime after lifetime, and in that role it has slowly gathered strength as the driving force of your earthly lives. As such, it has done an overall good job. However, the voice of the ego is also used to raising the alarm. As a built-in mechanism for survival, it is used to criticizing your actions, to questioning your decisions and to be judgmental of you as an individual. This criticism is part of its nature. It pushes you to self-examine and to self-improve in order to 'stay on top of the (so-called) food chain'.

Even though continuous review and judgment of self serves a purpose in the quest of survival, it can overstay its welcome when it starts to overly criticize oneself. As such, your ego voice can get out of hand, causing more harm and dissatisfaction if not counterbalanced with the protective loving voice from within. The ego may overwhelm you with thoughts of negative self-judgment, of not being deserving enough, of intense shame, self-hate or simply not being good enough.

When these thoughts of guilt and deep shame start to repeatedly present themselves, one needs to be reminded that the purpose of your life is to find deep and lasting love and joy, which starts with finding the deep appreciation and acceptance of love towards oneself.

Therefore, in order to offset the criticizing voice of the ego, it is of extreme importance that the protective loving voice from within is heard, acknowledged and listened to. And it's only through regular practice of meditation and reconnecting with this loving guidance from within, that you can become fully aware of its support, and embrace the realization that you are much greater than what your ego gives you credit for.

And as we have observed, this is where some of you instantly lose faith. This is where your ego immediately tries to intervene and erode your longing for greater meaning and purpose. This is where the ego tries to sabotage the need for spiritual connection – where it will argue with you, trying to convince you that only reason and logic are needed to secure a meaningful and happy life. The ego will try to install the belief that security within the physical realm, as well as entertainment and wealth, are the highest rewards to life. That happiness will be achieved through attaining the next physical goal, followed by another one, and another one, and another one. It will dismiss each achievement as yet another stepping stone in the never-ending ladder to 'success', and try to convince you that enough is never really enough because meaning and happiness will always lie a few more steps away.

And all this time you are deceiving yourself, as all that you desire is right here, in the very moment of the now. In the essence of your being. The perfect 'you' is right here. What you mostly desire is right here. It is accessible every moment, of every day, through stillness and quiet meditation. In the authentic consciousness of your being, where the thoughts that you are not good enough, simply fade. Where the feelings of shame, hurt or anger, will be exposed as an ego-constructed lie. Where the truth can be found – the truth that you are beautiful and deserving, and loving, and kind, with unlimited capacity for eternal love and grace.

This is where one can request to be supported. This is where one can request to be submerged in the soothing and protective rays of the Divine light. To see and feel it wash over you, embracing you, supporting you, protecting you, as one deserves. This is where one can ask for the deep wounds of the ego to be healed – where old and recurring pain and grief can be relieved, handed over to the angels of light, taken away in the eternity of love and grace. This is where difficult obstacles can be removed – where unlimited support can be received. This is where one can call upon an unconditional loving blessing, in the knowing that the gateway to love for self finally has been opened.

And as you embrace the authentic consciousness of your being, and surrender to the support and love of the Divine, your life will expand accordingly. It will unfold exactly as you desire it to, in knowing the truth: that you deserve the very, very best.

Only if one truly understands and accepts who one really is and attains a deep love and acceptance of self, is one living in alignment with the purpose of their lives. It is when this deep love towards oneself has been truly felt and accepted, that one realizes the true connectedness with all other human beings: friends and enemies alike. It is when you apply ultimate kindness and love towards the unique human manifestation of the Divine Consciousness you are, that love can truly be extended to others.

True love of self is the only way forward – for you as an individual as well as humanity at large. Love of self should never be mistaken for selfishness, which is ego-driven and aims purely at selfish and external rewards, often at the ruthless expense of others.

The focus of loving oneself needs to be on honoring the essence of who you really are, of remembering the love and goodness you were created from, of acknowledging the deep love that lies within, rather than enriching oneself with monetary and material gains at the expense of others. Loving oneself centers around a true appreciation of the expansive virtues you have been given, such as: kindness, patience, simplicity, (self) respect, forgiveness, gentleness, compassion, humility, joy and care. It is in line with these virtues that you are deserving of a great life, that you allow others to treat you with respect and show great respect for others. It is in line with these qualities that you are supported by the appropriate level of material goods to warrant this deserving life. Because once this true acceptance, embrace and authentic love of self has been found, appropriate rewards and physical support will flow into one's life.

For those of you who have been denied love in earlier parts of life, it is of great importance to acknowledge that you are completely loved and deserving of the all-encompassing love.

It is now that you need to be aware that every moment in your earthly life provides you with the opportunity to choose. Your task is to always choose love over fear, starting with allowing a deep acknowledgment and appreciation and love towards oneself. Treating oneself kindly and lovingly is your number one step in creating a happier and more peaceful and rewarding life. In opening the doors to self-love, you allow the Divine support to embrace you and allow new opportunities to come your way.

If a true deserving of self-love is reached at the highest and purest level, the manifestation of love will appear in the individual's life and situations of suppression, violence, poverty and malaise will change for the better. A deep sense of true deserving and knowing that one is part of the Divine will manifest in the individual's life, expressing itself through ultimate gratitude, happiness and joy. This sense of deserving will then naturally extend to others, reaching out beyond the self, in support of all others and all.

THE CRITICIZING VOICE OF OTHERS

The criticizing voice of others is often, at its core, the criticizing voice of you. By allowing the criticism of others to affect one's emotional state, one is in fact allowing oneself to criticize oneself. Each criticizing voice of the other needs to be examined in the context of one's view and condemnation of self – in one's shame of self. Each interpretation of the word of the other, more often than not, is the interpretation of one's own word to self.

The criticizing voice of others often triggers one's deepest emotional wound. As the ego tends to prevent painful events from recurring, the very thought of avoiding the painful event can, at times, attract a similar situation into one's life. There's a tendency for you to selectively hear comments, to hear the ones that reaffirm your emotional wound. You need to be aware that you are inclined to interpret situations negatively, because of these earlier painful events. You may have felt abandoned before, you may have been lied to, abused or made to

47

feel worthless. The comment from the other may trigger your emotional response, when in truth the comment may have had nothing to do with you. Being aware of your emotional wound, and realizing that the voice of others may have nothing to do with you, may help you on the journey to more self-love.

May I use the metaphor of a hot stove here: Your emotional wounds, caused by unfortunate events in life that have impacted you deeply, can be considered 'hot stoves'. And these hot stoves can be fueled by criticizing and negative ideas, either from self or others. In continuing the analogy, one can easily burn oneself on a stove if care is not being taken. Such it is also with the criticizing word of others in relation to your emotional wound.

As per manifestation design, the criticizing voice of others can form an important element in the growth of each individual on the path to self-love. Reflecting on a criticizing voice in relation to one's wound can be of momentary importance, in fairness towards self and the other. However, one does not need to get stuck into an ongoing cycle of criticism and negative thoughts, whether from others or self. One cannot allow the repeat of negative thoughts and criticism within their own mind as this only reaffirms the wound and trauma, rather than move on from it and heal. Just as one does not keep scratching a physical wound once it has been tended to, so one must guard against the repeat of negative thoughts, or allowing continuous criticism from others. One can observe the validity of the criticism, and possibly make a change. However, one then needs to move on from the criticism fast, and return to renewed grounds of self-love and self-support.

The risk of allowing the criticizing voice of others to repeat over and over again is that one can easily develop feelings of hatred towards oneself. These feelings of despising oneself can run very, very deep.

One needs to remember that one can turn a stove higher or lower. If you allow more fuel, it will get hotter and hotter. However, you can also decide to turn it down, or to switch it off completely. Allowing the repetition of negative and criticizing voices is like fueling the stove continuously. Breaking away from the ongoing negative ideas towards self, or from others, is like switching off the stove.

Unfortunately, the criticizing voice of others (and self) can be found in nearly every situation and will often be there in one form or another, if you allow it. Your individual growth comes from seeing the criticizing voice of others (and self) for what it is – just fuel for a stove, on which you can decide to burn yourself or not.

And as you don't spend your entire life right next to a hot stove, you do not have to surround yourself with the criticizing voices of others, nor the criticizing voice of self. You often have a choice – to either spend time in another room, or leave the home and enjoy your life outside, in nature, in another country, with yourselves or with others. Each one of you has a choice to follow a path that you create in loving support of yourself, in line with your passions and in happiness and joy.

And if the problem becomes too large, one can request help. The stove can also be replaced by another one, a gentler one, a safer one... one that doesn't burn you. It's part of the journey of your lives to recognize the hot stoves in your lives, and to always act out of deep love for self and see them for what they are. To realize that they will always be there in some shape or form, but that one does not to 'feed them with more fuel', nor let them become a source of torture or pain.

It is in your power to maneuver your lives away from repeated painful situations, to ask for help when needed, and to act in love and support of yourself. The criticizing voice of others only needs to be given attention when unavoidable or highly needed, and always with the utmost respect for self and protection of self as well as others.

You must always remember that you are deserving of complete love. Attaining true love for yourself requires measures of protection and accepting your true voice of being. Allowing sincere love and embracing the authentic self no longer has room for the repeated criticizing voice of others, or for the feelings of shame, despise or hatred they may cause.

And if you have truly made grave mistakes, you have to forgive yourself and allow for loving actions of redemption rather than holding onto self-blame and retribution. You are expected to fulfill your life passion and create the joyful life that you are intended to manifest. Transforming the attained self-love into a love of all others is then the automatic extension of the true purpose of one's life.

DENOUNCING SITUATIONS OF ABUSE

Not one individual deserves, or should ever stay in, abusive situations or relationships. Abusive relationships can be multi-layered and complex in their existence. One can perceive the abuse as a normal state of being, since it has repeated itself throughout their lives as a recurring wound that keeps being reopened and relived. Even though deep down you may be aware of the gravity and hurt of the abusive situation, you may believe it to be 'normal' as you have never experienced a more loving and joyful manifestation in your life.

However, deep within, you know the situation not to be right. Deep within, you long for a better and more loving life. Yet at times, you may decide to settle for less, as the notion that you are truly and deeply deserving of a better life has not manifested itself in its completeness yet.

You can easily feel discouraged about ever seeing a light in your dark circumstances. Yet, I want to assure each and every one of you that a better and more loving and fulfilling life lies around the corner. That once again, you are deserving of it. That each and every one of you is encouraged to go within and reconnect to the loving support that lies within and to call upon the Divine support to help you manifest a more rewarding life. A life of joy and loving support.

It is through this knowing, through this deep sense of deserving, and through your commitment to self-love, that you need to prioritize your wellbeing and gain the strength to start making changes in your situation. To realize that enough is truly enough and that you are deserving of a beautiful life.

Self-loathing, or detesting of self, can accompany the abuse, whether as perceived through the eyes of the abuser, or through the eyes of the victim. The origins of the self-revulsion or self-hatred need to be examined in order to allow oneself to move from the situation of abuse. The idea that somehow you could not be deserving of ultimate love, happiness and joy, needs to be replaced with a deep knowing that it is your birthright to be loved – by self as much as the other. It's your birthright to be treated respectfully and with integrity. It is your birthright to break the cycle of abuse. It is your right and your true destiny to live a loving and rewarding life, filled with joy, support and meaning, and on purpose. Each and every one of you is deserving of the very best life one can manifest.

You are Divine essence and you are supported. Listening to the truthful inner instruction when experiencing moments of abuse is of lifesaving importance.

One needs to always be aware that one is deserving of fulfilling one's purpose in life. That one is expected to express ultimate love for self, that one is expected to respect oneself above anything else. So that the true love of self, can eventually be extended to others. The strong awareness that the situation of abuse is not serving the individual or the highest good of humanity, and that you need to be removed from the abusive and harmful situation, needs to be prioritized. You need to find the strength to stand up for yourself and find the love that each child of the Divine deserves.

You should never make excuses for an abuser, and you should never allow abuse to occur out of sorrow for the abuser. Self-love, and placing oneself in a loving and safe situation, should always prevail before the hand of love can be extended to the other. The abuse should never be perceived to be out of love. It never is. As in a state of total acknowledgment of deserving the very best, the individual needs to continue calling upon the Divine support, and rather than request, you need to will a manifestation of change – a will based on the knowing that you are completely deserving. Your voice will be heard, as will for love is the will of the Divine Consciousness and it will always be supported. You have the right to stand up for yourself.

Standing up for yourself should always be in line with behaviors stemming from the Divine, such as: courageousness, compassion, empathy, truth, discernment, empowerment and respect. Expressing yourself with these behaviors in mind is a desirable way of facing your dilemmas when standing up for yourself and terminating conflict. Knowing that your conduct is in line with the consciousness of the Divine will mean you exude confidence, love and conviction. An effective way of asserting yourself will follow, therefore creating a safer and more protected situation.

Support may arrive through favorable situations, through like-minded individuals or important insights. Staying attuned to the inner voice and responding to its instruction will be desired. The most favorable plan of action will be given.

Some may call changes in the manifestations of their lives 'miracles'. Others may call it Divine interference. The strength of the Shared Consciousness, when willed upon, can set in motion changes – changes for the better. Whether small or large, when these 'breaks' present themselves, you are required to grab the Divine hand of assistance and move away from the situation of abuse, to a better manifestation of life.

Awareness of abuse as done to others should raise alarm and evoke action from each individual aware of the circumstances, with the purpose of ending the abusive situation. The care for others extends to all of humanity and involves awareness, action, unconditional love and dedication to a betterment of humanity.

Any interpretation of the Divine Word that entices abuse, or claims to be punishing in its nature, or entices violence in any shape or form, is man-made and has no relation to the all-encompassing love of the Divine Truth.

LESS, IS NEARLY ALWAYS, MORE

Happiness and joy lie within the simple gifts of life. Life was never intended to be complicated. Yes, you are encouraged to live your lives to your full potential, but the principles and values that lie at the root of joy in your physical manifestation are straightforward and uncomplicated. Unfortunately, you have forgotten about elementary simplicity. You have forgotten about the state of being and absorbing the free gifts of life.

Being with you, being with your fellow human loved ones, being in grace, with nature, in stillness and gratitude – these precious moments of unassuming joy are our biggest gifts to you. They anchor you into who you really are, into your connection to the consciousness of all that is – the birds, the trees, the waterfalls, the oceans, you, our beloved human beings. I cannot state it enough: you are all part of this One Great Love. And reconnection to that love, and knowing its full potential, is now a priority.

In order to achieve a healthier and happier life for all, and in support of a healthier planet, you are all advised to take a slight step back and reconsider the choices in your lives. Rather than producing more, there is an urgent need to start producing differently, with a different mindset. And it requires important changes on an individual level first. Let me explain.

The need to take a step back away from the treadmill of your modern day lives, and create quiet time, is now greater than ever. You are all on a fast ride to seemingly nowhere – producing more and more tangible elements of manifestation, which pollute your lives and your planet, rather than to enhance it. Many of you focus on the material achievements of life, much to the detriment of the inner rewards of the soul, which leaves you with profound hollowness and sadness, often questioning the purposes of your lives. From what we observe, your physical and technological impulses are constant and on all levels, with the fear of falling behind and losing out nearly as great as the fear of being alone. This fear of being alone has only increased due to the diminished sense of spiritual connection and of true belonging – a sincere loss of home.

Many of you are living a frantic and hectic life. This is like living under the constant stretch of a bow. Even though the continual surge of adrenalin works as an addictive mechanism, eventually the tension will erode your sense of being, and the string will snap, bringing along devastating consequences.

Currently, your material distractions are ample and follow each other at high frequencies. The delusion of material distractions and the suggestions that they bring you joy and happiness are an absolute farce. An over-indulgence in material possessions does not provide you with increased happiness. Fast entertainment and physical distractions do not fulfill the longings of your souls. Many of you are aware of it, yet struggle to find the answer or make the change, when really, the answer is very simple – it's right in front of you. Less is, mostly always, more. Less production, less consumption. More time to enjoy the simple gifts of life. In line with that, I state again: salvation does truly lie within. The quiet mind, the repetitive actions of a simple task, moments of stillness, all open the gentle path to a more meaningful existence, to greater happiness and peace.

You have no problem understanding that your much-beloved devices need frequent recharging to function as intended – the more frequent and intense the usage, the more the requirement to recharge the device. Your most important device however – the Divine body that carries you through the experiences of your life – is subject to a far more intense usage than it was many lifetimes ago. Your senses are bombarded with impulses that never stop. The drain on your energy source has intensified at an exorbitant rate, and the need to recharge frequently is now much greater than ever. Your night-time sleeps are, by far, insufficient.

Moments of true stillness, of quiet appreciation and gratitude for all the free things in life, are needed throughout your days; this is not only to recharge your body and minds, but also to remind yourselves of who you truly are and why you are indeed here. The capability to align yourselves with your soul's desire and intent, the capacity for salvation, lies within.

This is when you rediscover that the Shared Consciousness is the home where you left from, to experience your journey of earthly experiences. This is the home where all are still watching – the Divine support anticipating with you, guiding you. Wanting you to feel joy while you fulfill your purpose, of helping humanity evolve. Of helping you to realize ultimate love, of self and others, before eventually returning home. With your experiences, your moments of growth, your stories of joy.

In order for us to guide and assist you, you need to create the space and time to hear us. If you keep turning up the noise, and allow the constant distractions in your life without recharging on a regular basis, your guiding voice, your Divine network of support, won't be heard. Your answers won't come. Your path in life will feel devoid of meaning, and unclear in its unique purpose.

Embracing the simple gifts of life, turning down the noise and sitting in quiet meditation are first steps to increased healing of you and humanity at large.

FROM BOREDOM TO INSPIRATION

Currently, many of you have great concerns about the so-called state of 'boredom', when few quite understand that moments of boredom are no more than creations of the ego, regarding expectations towards the outer manifestation of life. In truth, moments of perceived boredom are precious moments of stillness that can be considered a gift – a moment in life where nothing is all, an opportunity for you to tune into the shared consciousness and sense the suggestions it has for your life. Please be aware that not one precious moment in your earthly live is a waste, and moments experienced as stagnant are essentially of great importance. Not only do they provide the crucial opportunity to connect to the wisdom within; they support increased intuition and awareness, and open the path for more inspiration, guidance and new directions in life.

Moments of so-called boredom can serve as the propeller of a readjustment on your path. Even though these moments can be misunderstood as bouts of nothingness and lacking direction, the opposite is true. A subconscious recharge and reactivation can take place, pushing you with renewed force into the path to follow. Embracing the moments of 'boredom', and using the time to go within, allows the stillness to speak and inspire. Renewed vigor and a decision to act can be important consequences.

One of your earlier greats, the brilliant Albert Einstein, acknowledged the importance of his intuition when working on his theory of relativity, receiving important information through intuitive and inspirational dreams. Academic and creative minds have been given crucial elements of important works through expanded awareness and their ability to tune into the creative source.

Putting in the request for Divine inspiration and support will be heard and answered. Ideas will be given and creative manifestation will be supported, step by step. Focusing on the task at hand and not letting distraction divert you from your creative intention will be beneficial in achieving your goals. The delicate sounds of life can only be heard when listened to with great attention, in stillness and reflection.

CREATING WITH AN INSTANT REWARD

One is encouraged to remember that great joys come from elementary actions, such as: working the soil, tending to gardens, harvesting, creating art and artifacts, creating tools, spending time in nature, educating, parenting, tending to the sick, and giving love, kindness and care to others.

In looking back at the concept of the instant reward: your ancestors sharpened their arrows, wove their baskets, sewed their clothes, built their shelter, herded their animals, gathered their fruits, built their fires and shared their knowledge, their stories and dreams. This instant reward from their actions was a gratifying element of their souls' desires, as it involved manifestation and creation. Their gains were instant and could be linked as a direct and immediate result from their actions. They celebrated the connection to the Divine through simple rituals and celebrations. These very acts of creating, honoring and observing life, as well as sharing of experiences and contributing to the wellbeing of others, still satisfy your souls.

The satisfaction from your creation, or the direct contribution to humanity, are still the major factors that fulfill the essential desires of your souls – the elements that bring you happiness and joy. It is your life's purpose to create, to contribute and to manifest. It's inherent in your life's journey to invent, construct and conceive of ideas that not only assist you and better your lives, but also the life of the tribe, and in a larger sense, one's humanity.

As your economies and technologies have developed, and mass production has increased, your instant gains have slowly been replaced by fragmented and distant rewards. Contributions (to the production) are compartmentalized, and the end result can't always be seen. Many workers are disconnected from the soul reward of seeing their contribution come to fruition. In many cases the contributions one makes are also those of negativity in that they contribute to pollution, abuse or the eventual destruction of humanity and the planet you inhabit.

Careers are planned with a long-term view in mind and shelter is paid off over a lifetime. Payment occurs in the future, and is experienced as detached from the actual work. These disconnected and distant rewards have removed many of you from the gratifying and direct link between positive creation and direct benefit and soul reward, leaving you with hollow longing and a general sense of dissatisfaction.

Therefore, and regrettably, the rate of mass production has disconnected many individuals from the satisfaction and gratification of the creative act. Over time, individuals have been placed as links in the chain of production, hence destroying the joy and purpose of large parts of the human experience, leaving many individuals apathetic and depressed. As your paths in life have expanded and increased in complexity and pace, what should not be forgotten is that the simple act of positive creation and contribution, and the subsequent soul reward, still hold one of the most important keys to purposeful and happy living - even if the acts at times could be considered mundane.

Nowadays, the instant reward also comes from the direct contributions one makes to the wellbeing of humanity when, for example, one researches within the medical, scientific or technical fields – when one produces products or services that help humanity to advance, without tarnishing its wellbeing. Even though the final reward from actual research may be in years to come, each step contributed to the positive research is a step in contributing to the wellbeing of humanity.

However, when research takes place with the destruction of humanity, or the demise of the planet in mind, individuals will eventually be filled with soul regret and one's conscience will be burdened vastly.

Therefore, reintroducing activities with a connection between creation and reward, which contribute to the health and prosperity of humanity, will increase the wellbeing and soul satisfaction of the individual as well as humanity at large.

AVOIDING THE TRUE TRAP OF CONSUMERISM

Your most 'advanced' societies, at their highest rate of materialistic consumption, experience most loneliness and despair within the souls of their people. From our angelic realms we observe deep sadness within these communities. We hear screams of despair, for all the wealth and consumerism have not brought happiness or fulfillment.

The notion that mass production and overconsumption contribute to a happier world is therefore a complete farce. Not only is the devastation of natural resources and habitat of flora and fauna of immense regret, but also the hollowness and dissatisfaction it leaves within humanity is of great concern. In order to determine whether mass production is a necessity within some of your industries, the determining factor should always be the wellbeing of humanity, rather than the monetary argument of corporate profits, greed and shareholders' gains. The primary consideration should always be welfare of the community and the need for authentic contributions by the individual, combined with shared soul rewards.

Immediately linked to the mass production of unnecessary and damaging goods is the falsely created urge to consume. In most cases, this urge is no more than a burning desire for a soul-fulfilling reward, since this gratifying part of creation is lacking throughout. Therefore, consumerism is no more than an attempt to band-aid the true hollowness inside. Unfortunately, consumerism can never replace the longing for true purpose within. It can never provide the gratifying soul reward one receives from contribution and creation, even though advertisements may try to install a different kind of belief.

Advertising campaigns are designed to brainwash, rather than to convey any sense of true desire or meaning. The picture of the ideal life cannot be shown in one frame, as life flows and moves and operates on different levels of emotion and being. The dynamic of ever-evolving life and one's unique contribution to it, is what provides the joy. Watching others exude a happy external life in a two-dimensional sphere, whether through your devices or via billboards and magazines, has no relation to the truth of happiness and joy. It is the actual doing and the accomplishment of the execution of ideas, as well as the possible learning from it, that brings true happiness and joy. Believing that the 'ideal' picture on the billboard or device holds any truth to happiness in life, is like believing that one is pasted against a wall, staring into space, never to move again. Please open your eyes to the current bombardment of impulses and advertising campaigns that have nothing to do with who you are. They are in complete contrast to where your vast potential lies and the true happiness that can be achieved.

Many of the current 'happy snaps' and advertising campaigns are designed to keep an economy alive, based on greed and false truths. This may come as no surprise, however many of you, despite the knowing, allow yourselves to be carried away by this stream of malady and decay. Many of you allow yourselves to feel inferior and sad if a similar external standard of perceived happiness and joy cannot be achieved. The need to stop comparing oneself to the outer display of others is urgent and imminent. The need to turn off your devices is real. Instead, the focus needs to be on the true gifts of life: the love and beauty that surrounds you; your loved ones close by; the creations that bring you joy; the experiences that make you soar; the activities that bring you closer to who you are.

Buying goods, just for the instant thrill it gives, does not increase your sense of happiness; it never has, it never will. The opposite applies in that it gives humanity a hollow sense of satisfaction and a loss of true purpose in life. How often have you purchased items, only to discard them after a certain amount of days? How often have you repurchased, only for the satisfaction and instant gratification it brings? And each and every time, the satisfaction fades. And left with it all is an ever-increasing toxic environment and an endlessly growing pile of harmful waste.

The constant comparison to others, combined with the over-consumption of unnecessary goods, as well as a worldwide destruction of nature, results in thoughts of depression and behaviors of despair. Placing the desire for happiness and purpose outside the individual, rather than within, defies all purpose and meaning and diminishes the point of life.

Again, creative activity is needed – doing rather than viewing, experiencing rather than buying, purposeful contributions rather than takings – to counterbalance the lack of soul satisfaction as a result of your current economic model... whether these soulful activities involve sustainable production of goods, the tending of gardens, the care for the other, the building of shelter, the research of matter, the climbing of mountains, the activity of sport, or the creation of art. The acts of creation and contribution are still vital keys to your happiness and the enrichment of your soul.

The incorporation of these activities into your daily lives enhances your sense of wellbeing and brings you in touch with the essence of who you truly are: part of the Creator who manifests and creates in line with the consciousness of the Divine and according to their soul's desire. Aligning your activities with a sustainable goal in mind, while sharing resources with the earth and your tribe, deepens the sense of achievement and soul reward.

THE UNIQUE CONTRIBUTION

From the angelic realm, we observe so much misguidedness and anguish, because the understanding of your true purpose and the connection to your soul power, in serving humanity and each other, has been lost.

Please be aware that you are not expected to save humanity all by yourselves, but it is part of your soul's journey and the purpose of your lives to contribute to the wellbeing of yourselves, your nearest and dearest, and humanity at large. It can be as simple as lifting someone's spirit, as being kind or extending a helping hand. There is such kindness and love to be given and to be received, yet so many of you keep closing off from it, choosing to distrust one another rather than to embrace.

It has been observed that many amongst you keep missing the simple opportunities for growth and joy. Instead, we observe that one cocoons oneself on the highway of life, more and more closed off from your fellow human beings. One needs to remember that if God had intended you to always communicate via a device, She would not have given you a body.

The physical experience of your human incarnation is still one of utmost importance, of purpose and grace – to look in the eye of the other and to connect with whom they are, to simply smile at your fellow human beings, to extend a helping hand, to assist in small ways. One needs to be aware that the biggest joys of all hide in the simplicity of life. The free life – the small acts of giving, the humble expressions of love, the gestures of support, the joy one brings to others. All of these offerings are part of the unique contribution one can make. They assist in the joy of others as well as the joy one brings to self, and to humanity at large.

Additionally, there's a plan for each one of you to serve humanity with your unique set of skills and affinities. Your unique contribution: in joyful spirit, with laughter and play and creativity. The compass to your unique contribution throughout your life lies within. In the consciousness of your being. In the template of your creation. The quiet traits of your personality, the affinities that inspire and elate. The little quirks you have. The very essence of you, just as you *are*. The activities you love; the compassion you feel. Your unique contribution springs forth from these distinct aspects of your being: the core of who you are, the imprint of your soul, you.

As you travel the path of your earthly existence, some of you may have doubts regarding the discovery of one's unique contribution. The path can be overshadowed by uncertainty and impatience, and the question of what one's true contribution may be can be confusing and overwhelming. Do not despair, as one of your popular expressions state: "Rome was not built in one day".

Additionally, one needs to remember that every small action, each minute creation and every interaction with another human being, will be part of the contribution one makes at any given time during one's life. Each act of kindness, each lending hand, each loving gesture, each generous smile, is part of your unique soul's imprint into the physical manifestation of your lives.

In simple terms, your unique contribution doesn't have to come in one large trophy deed. Your contribution can hide in an accumulation of the smaller acts of life. Also, there's no solid timeframe for the manifestation of one's unique contribution and one needs to remember that no effort, no activity, no learning, is ever lost. Skills and knowledge gained and acquired early on in life may be needed for contributions later. Therefore, every moment of one's life is valid and important, no matter how stagnant or disheartening a situation may appear or be perceived. The lessons learned, the skills gained, the love grown, will assist in the unique contribution one does make.

Therefore, hope is never lost. The one who followed the wrong path and caused pain and suffering in the past may gain insight into the effect of their actions and change their life for the better. They may redeem themselves by giving support, love and advice to those tempted to also follow the undesirable paths in life: such as choices of self-destruction, harm to others, or actions to the detriment of the wellbeing of the planet. As a result, and despite their unfortunate choices of the past, the unique contribution of the one who committed undesirable deeds, may consist in spreading the message of choosing right over wrong and pursuing a life of meaning over a life of hopelessness and despair. Their unique contribution may be in setting an example of change, of helping others to see the better life, of helping them on the path to self-love – to assist them in increased love for others and to help them change their lives for the better.

Each individual is advised to not cover their joy with a stream of negative thoughts, anxiety or fear. You are encouraged to relax more and put more trust into the notion that life will expand as per Divine design, once you put your true intention and desire into loving practice. Each appropriate action will then be followed by a fitting reaction, just as growth follows from seed – in the right spot, at the right time, without too much intervention and with a touch of tender love and care. So it is with your life. The physical manifestation of you will blossom, if you let it. If you nurture it, according to its true nature and desires, in alignment with Divine Awareness and Truth. In that, you are deserving of the most loving and joyful manifestation of your life.

Each and every one of you is encouraged to embrace the abundant gifts you have been given: the free gifts of life. To utilize your skills and learn from every situation that presents itself. To express and create, no matter how small the idea. To enjoy the right to feel loved, by self and by others, and the right to express and expand your love and joy. Most of what one truly needs is provided for, and one is only required to open up to all that has been given.

Go within, and know yourself. Appreciate and love yourself. Acknowledge your truth and your Divine origins. Recognize your unique skills and capabilities, your joys and authentic desires – every aspect, large or small. Feel gratitude for what you have been given, for the things that are working in your life. Your biggest handicap or regret may prove to be your largest asset. Embrace who you are – your little quirks and idiosyncrasies, your foibles and strengths – and live your life accordingly. Honor your own unique design, as per your unique path, in kindness and with love, and contribute accordingly – in small ways, or large ways, step by step, day in, day out, with the full awareness of who you are and with the support of the Divine Consciousness that has your back. It will support you, it will guide you, as soon as your call is placed and the right intention has been set. Go within, and listen. Ask and it will be given.

CHOOSING THE RIGHT THOUGHTS

When the ego is presented with sadness or despair, sometimes it may appear that it's hard to focus on the grace of the Divine, especially when those feelings overwhelm you. It needs to be remembered that at such moments it is often the personality which is wounded. The story of the ego, the one you have been identifying with, is the one mostly causing the suffering. Personality, or the ego, is like the story you have been creating throughout your life. It contains the elements that can be added to the resumé of your life: the aspects of the outer appearance, the elements of the outer body and its achievements – everything that can be observed and categorized in physical terms, by you and by others.

The voice of the ego can create a lot of noise in one's day-to-day life, and it's only while being still and in a situation of quiet contemplation that you can recognize the actual thoughts that create the turmoil in your life. It is then that you realize that all thoughts are flowing from your active brain – from the organ that serves the ego, the instrument that serves the physical existence, and generally, attempts to protect you from earthly harm and vulnerability.

As explained earlier on, it is the brain's job to review past experiences and anticipate future events. It brings you thoughts of past experiences, it interprets them and helps you assess and anticipate future events, so it can protect you from harm and anticipate your survival.

With the diminishment of daily natural threats to the human species, and the easier organization of your lives, your brains have developed over time. They have grown in certain areas, and diminished in others as per survival need. The capacity to interpret and explain physical reality has vastly increased.

However, since the brain has always been focused on protecting the physical manifestation of self and to always anticipate the looming threats, it is now more inclined to fight rather than to ease, to be aggressive rather than peaceful, to react from fear rather than love. It is more inclined to foresee disaster, rather than prosperity. In fact, the ego now finds it easier to entertain negative thoughts rather than positive ones, and entertaining these negative thoughts now requires less actual energy than allowing you to have positive ones. This is being witnessed on an individual level, as well as your humanity at large. As such, the negative thought patterns have established themselves well and truly in your lives and throughout the world - like loud unwelcome guests who visit regularly but do nothing other than lower the energy and darken the space. As such, the ego, with its thoughts, has moved further and further away from its initial intention: to support the manifestation of the virtues of Divine, within the physical realm.

Since you are part of the Consciousness which creates, your manifestation follows on from your mindset of intention and thought. As such, your ego needs to support the intention of the Divine, rather than work against it. Thoughts of shared love, of optimistic hope, of peace and wellbeing, of possibility and expansive creation, will allow the shared energy to rise and open up to more positive manifestations and creations in your lives – individually as well as globally. As stated before, each simple choice, each simple action, each thought in line with the Divine, will open the path to the manifestation of a more loving, joyful and happier humanity. It is of lifesaving importance that one selects and directs their thoughts as promisingly and confidently as possible to allow love, peace and joy to support the new direction of your lives, and that of humanity at large. The qualities of the ego need to be redirected and used to their maximum capacity: in support of a better life and in line with the virtues of the Divine.

It requires focus, choice and determination to change your patterns of thinking. It requires raised awareness to focus on a creation of love and peace, of wellbeing and health. It is during times of quiet contemplation or meditation, when stillness is embraced, that you can observe your thoughts with more awareness. It is then that one realizes that certain thoughts can be entertained and given power to and that others can be let go of.

It is part of your spiritual journey to become aware of your patterns of thoughts and choose more positive ones into the reality of your lives – to allow expansive ideas over restricting ones, to allow possibility over unfeasibility, to welcome peace over war, and hope over despair. The way in which you choose the direction of your thoughts will assist in a better manifestation of your lives, making you the co-creator of your experiences and those of humanity at large.

To illustrate this point with a simple analogy, your thoughts and their reality can almost be observed like a highway from above. Your thoughts are needed in your physical world to get the progression of your lives from A to B. Like automobiles on a highway, your thoughts may come and go. They will move lanes, cause havoc, horns may honk and engines may be revved, but beyond all that frantic action lies the vast reality: the stillness of the earth, the peacefulness of the sky and the gently flowing air. The fields afar remain quiet and inviting in their beauty, and as you travel along, you have a choice. Either you can be stressed and bothered by the drama and chaos on this limited highway of life, or you could simply observe it for what it is, and consider it as a mode to get from A to B while still being aware of the vast beauty that lies above and beyond.

In the last case, you can then decide either to stay on the frenzied highway with its entrapments and disarray, or leave the route and choose a calmer and slower path where beauty can be observed:

where birds fly, where the wind rustles the leaves in the trees, where the smells of nature will entice. And this choice of experience needs to be made by you; this choice of peace in your life is yours – the choice either to cut out the noise and stress by taking the calmer route, or staying on the frantic highway of life. Both ways will get you to your destination, but the experience of your journey will be vastly different.

And such it is with your choice of thoughts.

NEGOTIATING FEELINGS

Feelings are relevant, and acknowledging feelings is important since feelings are the meeting place of the reactions of the ego and the inner wisdom of the soul. Feelings are a response to the outer circumstances of life, as observed by the ego as well as the soul's indication that attention needs to be paid.

However, you are not your feelings. What you are is Divine potential and love.

When strong feelings occur, one needs to be reminded of the entrapments of the ego and remember their Divine essence. Staying calm in the midst of adversity and steering away from immediate ego reaction is part of your individual empowerment and your spiritual path in life.

Feelings of anger, sadness or frustration can be acknowledged and can be inwardly honored. Unless one is in a life-threatening situation, feelings mostly don't need an immediate reaction or response. As with thoughts, feelings can be acknowledged with the realization that they will come and go. Acknowledging feelings for what they are is a first step in coping with the outside world.

Validating the intensity of feelings is recommended as it can be an important mechanism for coping with the situations of life. However, one needs to remember that if acknowledged and accepted, feelings will eventually dissipate, after which an appropriate response can be received and formulated – a response based on the essence of love and respect as guided by the wisdom from within.

Such a response will then serve humanity and is in the best interest of all involved. Responding to feelings from the inner wisdom and shared consciousness is the way to achieve true peace, happiness and bliss.

At times, the human ego can perceive situations as volatile and threatening. Circumstances can evoke notions of panic and despair, of lost opportunities or simple thoughts of missing out. Please note that no-one ever truly misses out. Creation is abundant and provides for all. The key always lies within. One needs to have faith that in situations where certain opportunities are missed, new and sometimes better ones will soon arise. Stepping aside for another could be in the interest of self, even if advancements are not immediately noticeable. Decisions that burden one's conscience should not have to be made. More suitable and rewarding long-term gains will be in the making. Releasing oneself from the restricted view of one single desired outcome is therefore recommended.

Validating and accepting feelings, as well as formulating a response in line with the virtues of the Divine, is a vital part of living one's spiritual journey on earth and healing one's physical existence.

CREATING FROM THE NOW

One co-creates their reality by allowing and steering their thoughts and choosing one's response to feelings. As thoughts either reflect on past events, or relate to ideas and plans about the future, the peace and truth always lies within the now. The reality of the thought is that it is fleeting and based on perceptions and interpretations as determined by the ego. Therefore, one mostly has a choice, in the moment of the now, as to how to think and subsequently how to feel about a situation. Unless an immediately violent or extremely traumatic situation is being experienced or witnessed, one can mostly be selective in the choice of their thoughts. Thoughts can either supply one with energy or drain one's vitality. Ultimately one mostly has a choice, in the very moment of the now, as to how one responds to events. The personal response to events will affect one's experience of life.

If one chooses restrictive and negative thoughts, they will torment and exhaust. However, if one chooses positive or expansive thoughts, they will feed gratitude, peace and an appreciation of life. Every moment in the now is one of possibility. It provides the opportunity to observe and be in awe of all that is. Each moment, one can express gratitude for all the things that are, for all the potential that is. No matter how dire the circumstances, no matter how sad the situation appears, you still have a choice in how to respond emotionally and spiritually to the circumstances in which you find yourselves. Not that dire circumstances are desirable or need to be condoned.

The choice right now is to choose love over hate, forgiveness over resentment, hope over despair. Each choice of thought, in every moment of the now, is one of ultimate freedom of the soul. It is in this ultimate choice, on the fringe of all human manifestation, that Divine power can be found. This eventual choice, in line with Divine Grace, can never be taken from anyone. This is where one's final and all-encompassing freedom lies. It is one's ultimate power in the physical expression of the now, the return to one's Divine nature and truth, in line with all-encompassing love.

Unfortunately for many of you, the stresses and fears of day-to-day life overshadow this freedom of how to respond to your situation, and as a consequence many allow yourselves to feel sad and desperate within the experiences of your lives, right now.

I can almost hear one's earthy dilemma: "How can we anchor ourselves in the now, and choose love over fear, when life is so hectic? When we have a job to go to and a family to feed? There is only limited time, life just takes over..." Well, this is where one is required to practice stillness and observe the highway of one's life. This is where one is required to ask for guidance from within. What is it really, that keeps you on this chaotic road, on this fast and relentless highway of stressful living? What is it that keeps you from taking a slightly different turn? Maybe an alternative route that is slightly calmer, but ultimately more gratifying and rewarding. Is it the criticizing words of others? Or is it one's judgment of self? If so, why are you choosing to allow this negative self-judgment to happen?

Go within and listen with intent. Find the direction from your loving source. Listen and follow the cues to a happier and more rewarding life.

Spiritual growth occurs when the forces of your individual thoughts and choices are being aligned with the power of the Divine. The awareness and conscious choice of thoughts helps to recreate one's life for the better. Each consciously chosen constructive thought based on love, kindness, gratitude and appreciation will improve the individual's experience of life.

Conscious change of thoughts and actions 'en masse' changes humanity.

In this line of thinking, one needs to remember that past and future are no more than concepts, as created by the brain, to maneuver through the physical manifestation of life. This doesn't mean that the concepts of time don't serve a purpose within the earthly existence; they do, and as such they should be respected and honored.

However, in order to understand the depth of all-encompassing truth, one needs to remember that this always lies in the experience of the now. As you read these words, and without reference to past or future events, you may ask yourselves, what is my experience of the now, right now? In applying gratitude for all that is given – your food; your shelter; the functioning of your bodies; the intelligence of your brains; the beauty of a flower; the movement of a bird; the music in your ears; the vastness of the skies; the love and care for others; the potential for all that is – one will understand the truth.

The now is the only reality that truly holds. It's the true existence. True peace and wellbeing lie within the knowing of the now, without wallowing in thoughts of regret about the past or extreme concern about the future. The now is multi-dimensional and layered with levels of consciousness, with Divine power, and choice. Your soul fulfillment opportunities are vast and many choices can be made, but an important factor for you to remember is to experience joy – joy from a life that's in alignment with who you are, with your Divine purpose. A life of positive thought and creation, that contributes to the happiness of self as much as others. A life that supports humanity, and loves and respects one another, as well as the planet it inhabits.

Expanding one's love, gratitude and appreciation within the now raises the level of consciousness and brings reality into a higher vibration. The now therefore holds all potential. It holds complete capacity for love – love of self as well as love of others. To be anchored in the now, and to sense and know the powerful Divine potential that hides within it, is part of the spiritual human discovery and the path to complete happiness and peace.

Creation from the essence of the now has full potential to create a blissful and happy life, for all.

All potential to love, to create, to feel grateful, and to contribute lies within the consciousness of the now and starts with your intention and your choice of thoughts. It is within the acceptance and the embrace of the now that true empowerment lies. The choice of how to respond, no matter what situation one finds oneself in, is what leads to ultimate meaning. The free choice of contributing to the wellbeing of humanity springs forth from the awareness of the creative potential hidden in the now. In simple words, each moment in your physical lives offers a moment of choice. The choice to love (oneself and others), and to create and contribute in line with the virtues of the Divine, is the ultimate contribution one can make to the physical expression of life – to the manifestation of earthly creation. This is the ultimate path to living life on purpose.

Understanding that your full potential is determined by your conscious intention and choice of thoughts is part of the spiritual journey of life.

Choosing the right intention, in line with the Divine, will lead to meaningful and purposeful living as well as ultimate soul reward.

One needs to have faith that: 'the glass is always more full than empty'. One needs to remember that every negative thought is one of restrictive energy, ultimately diminishing one's full experience of life. Each choice of negative thought, and allowing its prolonged effect, can therefore be considered self-sabotaging in its nature. A positive thought however, is expansive in energy and will empower one's capacity to create, to contribute and experience happiness and joy. Being grateful in the now re-anchors one into the Consciousness of the Divine.

The choice between serving the purpose of your soul, rather than limiting your service to the needs of your physical self, is presented on a day-to-day basis. The growing awareness of the choice between these two is part of your spiritual path and growth. Learning to distinguish between Divine self and physical self, between Divine purpose and physical purpose, and aligning your physical actions with the virtues of the Divine – this is the reason why you are here. Choosing love over hate, peace over anger, compassion over judgment, right over wrong. Each situation, in each moment of life, is a moment of choice and therefore a moment of growth. Making the right choices, in line with the Divine, is why you are here.

PART 2 – HEALING HUMANITY

TIMES OF TRANSFORMATION

As your threat of worldwide war increases and the chance of total destruction of your precious planet grows, the need for the understanding of the shared connection to the Divine is now greater than ever – in order for humanity to survive, to achieve happiness, to heal, to progress, to learn and love. As discussed before, the vast absence of a true connection to the inner Divine is a tragic sign of your times. The current confined spiritual practice is too constrained in that it does not extend the spiritual practice and its application sufficiently into day-to-day life, and at times the goals of the religious institution, or segments thereof, surpass the Divine intent through focusing on ego-driven benefits.

Daily meditation, stillness or prayer are urgently required, whether this occurs in your churches, your synagogues, your mosques, your temples, or simply in nature or your homes. It has no real relevance where it occurs. The importance lies in the true connection and the awareness and the commitment of each individual to apply the virtues of the Divine Consciousness into daily life.

Your supportive Divine spark needs to shine in order to reach a level of happiness and joy that sustains a healthy and thriving humanity. A humanity where individuals can manifest true meaning and purpose within their physical lives. A humanity with an abundance of love and respect for all life on earth: your fellow human beings, your plants, your animals, the beautiful creation of your planet. A humanity which refrains from aggression, violence, neglect, oppression or wars. This can be achieved and this thriving humanity is the purpose of all human incarnations.

You may ask again, is it really possible? Humanity living in peace? Humanity acknowledging that all souls are connected and as part of one shared Consciousness, that all are living its virtues in each and every moment of their lives?

You may ask, how does that relate to the current lifestyles of many – the race for something better, the race for the next important thing, the world-wide pollution and the greed-driven activities of corporations? You may wonder about the stressful lifestyles, about poverty throughout the world, about economic competition and the need to advance the economy. You may wonder about mass consumerism and the stress of unemployment for many. You may wonder about the increase of violence as a consequence of some religious segments. Please know that most of these sad developments are self-induced and can be reversed swiftly, without the loss of life qualities. Please note that right choices can be made for all.

The first step needed is the denouncement of damaging dogmatic beliefs.

DAMAGING DOGMATIC BELIEFS – THERE IS NO WRATHFUL GOD

Beliefs that are passed down, generation after generation, without being questioned or adjusted according to the spiritual growth and understanding of your time, are considered dogmatic beliefs. Some of these dogmatic beliefs can have far-reaching damaging effects on the individual, as well as humanity in all its being.

Unfortunately, some segments of religious institutions interpret and entertain principles that can be considered damaging in their dogmatism. When these dogmatic ideas involve interpretations of Divine suppression or wrath, it needs to be understood that these principles are not flowing from the Divine Consciousness; rather they are man-made and ego-based. They mostly serve the power of the religious segment, rather than the authenticity of the true Divine message, which encompasses the message of unconditional love for all. There is no displeased or wrathful God. All of the Divine

Consciousness is unconditionally loving and supportive, and all of who you truly are is pure, and stems from this unconditionally loving Source.

The notion that human beings are somehow sinful, simply through their very existence, is not in line with the truth. The idea that as a consequence they are somehow deserving of punishment or abuse approaches the notion of evil ideas. Therefore, do not let these questionable sets of principles distract you from the path of love. In simple words, there is no punishing or wrathful God to be feared. Love is all there is. You have been created in the image of God, and you are all part of the one shared consciousness. All of the Divine wisdom and God's truth of love lies within each and every one of you.

History has unfortunately shown that some dogmatic ideas are being used and abused in the pursuit of power. Again, these damaging ideas are man-made and have no relation to the Divine essence of love. Some segments preaching these rigid and misinterpreted ideas can open the path to evil in that they can abuse, oppress, condemn, murder and cause war in the name of religion. This is of great sadness and concern as we observe that most of humanity's suffering is caused by this misuse and misinterpretation of the truth of love. One also needs to remember that those who wrote the texts in sacred books did so in the context of their time and their time restrictions, and through the eyes and understanding of a human being. Passed on over time and generations, distortions and inaccuracies in translations have not always been avoided.

The danger of some dogmatic ideas occurs when the goals of segments of a religious institution surpass the purity of the Divine message of love. The ego and power-driven desires of individuals representing segments of the religious institution suddenly become the focus of the religious activity, at the expense of others. As such, dogmatic beliefs have been, and are being misused as justifications for evil behaviors, often to the benefit and financial empowerment of individuals hiding behind the sacredness of the rest of the organization.

Physical and sexual abuse of children, women and men, as well as monetary abuse of funds, saddens the Angelic realm. Practices of extortion, suppression, ethnic cleansing, violence, murder and war are sadly, and tragically, committed 'in the name of God'. It leaves us with deep sorrow and intense grief to observe these evil practices based on the misuse and misinterpretation of the Divine message of love.

There is no wrathful God. There is no God who requires violence or oppression, murder or intimidation to make His point or keep humanity 'in line'. There is no God who encourages anyone to hate, bully, discriminate, torture, murder, or rape. There is no God who would spur anyone into being brutal, or slaughter the very own people She created and loves. God, the Divine Source of all, is one of unconditional love, no matter how you manifest as a human being in life: as to who you are, as to where you're from, as to what the color of your skin is, as to what sex or sexual orientation you may be. Rich or poor, you are all created in the image of the Divine.

You are all unique expressions of the Creator and you are all part of His Great Love, of Her Great Love. As such, you are all unconditionally loved and respected. No individual or group should ever be persecuted in the name of God. Rather, each individual, each group, is to be loved, celebrated and respected for their own uniqueness and manifestation. Because it is through their uniqueness that each individual contributes to the rich tapestry of life.

Divinity knows no evil. Your soul's purpose is to not only love yourself but also your fellow human beings, equally. Your path of spiritual growth is just that – spiritual growth. It reconsiders, it re-understands, it re-examines life in your growth and understanding of the truth. It applies the Divine virtues and understanding, without exemption and in full understanding of the truth, which constitutes an unconditional love for all.

The understanding from thousands of years ago is a sometimes narrower understanding due the limitations of that time. As a humanity, your understanding has since grown and you have spiritually developed. You are growing closer to the truth. As such, a more loving understanding of the truth is now being achieved and is much needed – an understanding that the Divine Consciousness is part of you all and that each and every one of you is an expression of unconditional love. Therefore, you should all be loved and embraced as you have been created. This understanding is to be reflected within your practice of prayer or meditation.

It has been observed that many of your prayers aren't resonating to large parts of the population since they're expressed through old languages and concepts. They can therefore be experienced as being abstract in their meanings, and difficult to relate to in your contemporary way of life. Therefore, for many, they can leave a large gap between your earthly existence and a true sense of Divine connection. Emphasizing the connection to the Divine within, and restoring faith in the closeness and availability of its support, will increase the faith for each individual and humanity at large.

FACING ONE'S CONSCIENCE

One's conscience is the eternal memory of all actions and reactions in the physical sphere.

Upon leaving the physical sphere, one faces their conscience in the presence of the great Creator. Facing one's conscience, while having been responsible for profoundly immoral acts which have caused harm, death or destruction of any of the Divine gifts, leaves one deeply saddened, expansively shamed and filled with profound regret.

Exercising one's power to abuse, hurt or humiliate your fellow human beings, or tarnish any of the creations of the Divine, can be considered evil acts. Even though a perpetrator may think that their earthly power leaves him untouchable, the sad eternal truth will be revealed upon leaving the earthly existence when one's conscience needs to be faced. No matter how much one tries to hide behind a powerful organization or institution, no matter how much one successfully lies or covers up, one will be faced with the individual choices as made in one's life, and the ultimate consequences of one's actions and deeds will be felt deeply and vastly by the perpetrator, and will burden her conscience immensely.

The consequences of evil actions or harm to others have therefore far greater effects on the perpetrator's soul, rather than the soul of the victim. Pain to others in the physical manifestation of life causes great pain, vast burden and deep profound grief to the eternity of the perpetrator's soul. As what one does to others is really done to self, the complete consequences and intense pain of evil acts towards an individual, or groups at large, will be deeply felt and experienced by the perpetrator. The overwhelming pain will be understood in its intensity and eternal effect, leaving the perpetrator's soul trapped in a deeply dark realm – one of profound sorrow, shame and regret.

Acts of kindness, caring and love are the only path to redemption of the soul. As such, the only reprieve from the consequences of one's action is the right choice, in line with the inner truth, when a situation occurs. Until right choices are made, one will face similar dilemmas over and over again, incarnation after incarnation. The consequences of the prolonged misunderstanding of the truth are that of prolonged soul suffering and entrapment, due to actions of non-love. One's conscience only releases and forgives when actions of expansive love have been expressed over and beyond, opening the door to the soul's redemption, releasing it slowly, into the vibration of the Divine.

Actions of love are exponential in their effect in that they counterbalance expansively the actions of hate. Therefore, each action of love, big or small, has a powerful flow-on effect to the wellbeing of humanity, even if the direct consequences cannot be observed immediately. Simple acts of kindness increase the level of vibration exponentially and therefore each individual has great capacity and power to contribute to a better humanity and a higher level of living in loving awareness.

War and hate can be counterbalanced by shared acts of love, as well as peaceful prayer and meditation. These shared calls for love will raise the shared awareness, diverting a situation from a threat of war to one of happiness and peace.

The simple acts of contributing to anyone's wellbeing, whether through material gifts or simple gestures of kindness and love, also bring one closer to the consciousness of love.

When acting in line with the Divine, and to the wellbeing of all, the Divine support will prevail. One's conscience will be clear.

EMBRACING THE TRUTH OF UNCONDITIONAL LOVE

The forces of love behind the Divine creature you are, are exponential and radiate well beyond the self. Truly embracing the unconditional love of the Shared Divine Consciousness brings the automatic understanding that one will never do to others what one doesn't want to be done to self, as you are all part of One.

Furthermore, all knowledge between right and wrong is well embedded within your hearts, and as you travel the path to greater love for self and others, you are faced with important choices along the way. Deep down, each one of you is aware of how to choose right over wrong. One knows how to prioritize the ethically and morally right choices in accordance with the voice of one's soul, as sensed from within.

The choices one makes in line with love will make a difference in your world. Each simple choice, each simple action, in line with the virtues of the Divine, will open the path to a manifestation of a more loving, joyful and happier humanity. As such, each individual choice or action will assist you in living your life on purpose and with true awareness and meaning.

There's no point in focusing on 'how wrong the other one is': a neighbor, an un-loyal friend, or that person from another culture or another race. Beneath the expressions of the ego, you are all One and you are created from love and kindness. Sadly, in the physical world, some of you may have lost their way, but there's no need for you to lose your way. There's no need for you not to follow the guidance of your inner compass.

The actions of your ego should always follow the directions of your inner voice, in order to fulfill your understanding of the truth and increase the wellbeing of humanity. Actions to cheat, lie, abuse, murder or betray, are misinterpretations from the ego, and are not in line with the fulfillment of your soul's purpose. So, immediate realignment is required. Actions in line with love – that cherish, respect, behave in honesty and with integrity, with courage and grace – are actions guided by the Divine and are in line with the soul's purpose, and therefore humanity's true destiny.

When in doubt, or if a situation doesn't appear right, one is encouraged to find a moment of stillness and go within. You will be instructed. You will be guided – whether one needs to move away from a business deal, or people who may harm you. When guidance is asked for, the answer will be given. As one practices more and more, the ease of recognizing the guiding voice will increase vastly.

TREAT YOUR NEIGHBOR AS YOURSELF

All of you, my beloved, are placed on this earth to rediscover and realign with the eternal good that is within each and every one of you, and that connects you all. You are all one. Therefore, view your neighbor, whether a friend or an enemy, as you view yourself, since you are your neighbor and you are your enemy, and you are also yourself. The notion of 'you' and 'them' has no relation to the truth in eternal life.

The obstacles you view towards your neighbor or your enemy are often a reflection of the obstacles you encounter within your own ego, as created by the repetition of your thoughts. Increasing the awareness of the obstacles as created by your ego is part of the purpose of your manifestation here on earth. Recognizing the obstacles aids you in acquiring spiritual insights. As you travel the path of life, the growth of spiritual awareness is directly related to what you encounter in the physical sphere and how you respond to it. Your purpose is to rediscover the goodness that lies within each and every one of you, and to realign your actions with the virtues of the Divine. With actions following on from that understanding, you will be able to contribute to a betterment of humanity.

As stated before, you are your neighbor, you are your enemy, you are your forests, you are your fauna. Treat all with the highest level of respect and love. Do not despair about suffering as I am guiding you to the path of decreased suffering. The very realization that it is possible for each and every one of you to achieve a state of graceful bliss is your purpose on this earth.

Humanity is under a lot of pressure, and the state of global animosity needs to end. Do not buy into the destructive and fear-driven thoughts and ideas that separate your shared humanity. Do not buy into the calls for war. Now is the time for each one of you to hold a deep inner vision of peace, respect and shared love in order to keep humanity on its path to increased wellbeing.

One cannot completely understand the apparent negative vibrations within the other individual, but as their path crosses yours, a response of love and an awareness that essentially you are all one and the same, will strengthen and enlighten you both. Please note, this does not mean that one shouldn't be held responsible for unjust actions, and your legal systems do have an important role to play in guiding unenlightened individuals into what is right and what is wrong. The challenge within each one of you is to not repay evil with evil, but rather overcome evil with good. A response of love is always leading the path.

Understanding the suffering of your fellow human beings and being able to help elevate some of the suffering is one of the ways forward, as only love will bring you the answer when faced with earthly struggles. The appearance of evil and suffering needs to be met by faith in love. A crucial element is to acknowledge love for self as much as love for others, since all were created out of love, and all, including self, are deserving of love.

In circumstances of intimidation or violence, one is required to go within and remember that one is deserving of love. One needs to remember the strength one has been given and tap into the capacity to stand up for oneself in a loving and deserving way. One needs to have faith that the Divine Consciousness will support and guide you to a betterment of the situation and change the experience from anguish, anger or despair, to love. Listen intently to the wisdom within, allow for timing, and recognize measures and changes in the experience of the situation that come your way.

Through daily meditation and prayer, and focusing on the virtues of the all-encompassing goodness of the One Great Love, you are living the Divine Truth and you will assist humanity on its path to wellbeing.

UNDERSTANDING THE NEMESIS

As stated many times before, each and every one of you, in human incarnations, are connected through the spinal cord of Shared Love and Divine Consciousness. Your nemesis is part of the same consciousness and therefore is part of you. On many occasions, parts of the nemesis can reflect some of the ego-driven behaviors of you yourself, containing attributes which you may wish to overcome. The nemesis can reflect the personality traits one struggles to face. However, overcoming these traits within the self often forms the milestones of spiritual growth. It's the opponent's behaviors which, rather than being criticized outwardly, should be examined inwardly. In that sense, every notion of disapproval, hatred or dislike, needs to be reconsidered and weighed up against the virtues of graceful discernment, understanding, compassion, forgiveness and love.

The finger one points at the other in judgment or disapproval is often a finger pointed at oneself. Go within and examine which part of the personality runs parallel with the observed behavior of the nemesis. This part of the personality is one for spiritual growth and improvement. "Let him who is without sin, cast the first stone". The honesty with which one can observe the behavior of the nemesis through the constructed ego of self, helps one understand the opportunities for spiritual growth.

The (perceived) darkest values of your nemesis will, in many cases, illustrate your most profound teachings. They communicate the path of life not to be traveled, and provide an opportunity to steer away from the shadows of the personality. When understood at the deepest level and contemplated in its truth, a profound shift will occur, replacing the shadow with the light. Compassion for the nemesis will grow and the attachment to judgment of the nemesis will diminish, opening the door to forgiveness and growth.

Forgiveness does not involve condoning the behavior of the nemesis; rather it centers round raising your own level of awareness and understanding from an ego level to a level of higher consciousness and love. In choosing to view the nemesis through the understanding of the higher awareness, the position of the nemesis will be viewed as limited in their ego-understanding and in much need of spiritual growth. Enveloping the nemesis with thoughts of expanding love carries the essence of forgiveness and will relieve you from your own suffering. Sending love, rather than hanging onto bitterness and hate, is therefore the fastest way to healing one's wound in relation to the nemesis. Without having to condone the actions of the nemesis, a strengthening of the soul through a deeper understanding will follow. The vibrational level surrounding the shadow's existence will be increased, clearing the way to an expansion of love and inner peace for all involved.

Spiritual growth lies within and will manifest outwardly. Knowing the truth (to the path of Divine Love) is an important purpose of your soul's incarnation, and increasing the overall vibrational awareness through understanding the truth is the path to saving humanity. Shifting the awareness from the physical level to a Divine understanding in each and every moment of one's life opens the path to the all-encompassing and Divine Truth.

The deep understanding that you are all part of the same Divine Consciousness, and the remembrance of that understanding when facing the nemesis, forms the sacred and Divine knowledge to the path of salvation and the saving of humanity. The understanding that one must never do to another what one wouldn't do to oneself, is the key to peaceful and purposeful living. Serving the other, as one would serve oneself and our loved ones, is the ultimate grace and soul fulfillment. The faith in this Divine path, and the commitment to expanding one's love, are the keys to purposeful living and understanding the truth.

As one incarnates, and incarnates again, one can manifest lives which operate at higher vibrational levels of consciousness, in turn raising the overall level of (Divine) awareness amongst humanity. It involves overall peace, true happiness and most of all, joy. Please be aware that living according to the Divine Truth involves vast and endless experiences of true joy. Continuous somber and austere contemplation, and forbidding and astringent living, are not a long-term goal in line with purposeful living. The true path revolves around vast joy, respect and love for all, including the planet and all inhabitants.

BUT, WHAT ABOUT VAST SUFFERING?

I am aware that, even though you find a lot of solace in my words, you are struggling with the notion of the vast suffering you witness around you in your earthly existence. You are wondering whether this widespread suffering was a so-called 'glitch' from your Creator? I hear you. I hear you wonder as to how an unconditionally loving consciousness can allow suffering amongst your fellow human beings?

Please be aware that suffering is not a matter of 'allowing', and with your concern about a 'glitch', this is not the case. All of earthly creation is part of the greater vision of spiritual perfection and ultimate love. As you are all part of the Divine Consciousness and all of you are connected, the suffering of each individual is in fact the suffering of all of humanity. The desire to relieve the suffering is currently experienced through the witnessing of the suffering. This, therefore, doesn't mean that the Divine Consciousness condones the suffering within the physical realm, as it is unconditionally loving and supportive of complete happiness and joy.

What needs to be remembered is that living in line with the Divine Consciousness requires one to contribute to the wellbeing of all of humanity. If truly and deeply understood, and if each individual lives according to this truth, all of humanity's suffering has the potential to end. If each and every one of you considered your neighbor, your nemesis and your sick and frail as if they were you yourselves, and in complete unconditional loving understanding and practice, suffering would be vastly alleviated and has the great potential to end.

Healthy food production and prevention of disease would have priority. Food would be equally distributed and shared. Medical knowledge would be respectfully shared amongst modern and traditional practitioners, between Western and Oriental sciences. Healing priorities would be set. Research into new medicinal healing solutions would be prioritized over research into new weaponry. One would be offered the best and most suitable medical treatment and one would be cared for.

One would stop the production of weaponry and lay down all arms. The wellbeing and happiness of all of humanity would prevail. Each individual would treat the other with kindness, compassion and respect. There would be no discrimination or intimidation. There would be no fighting or bullying or despising. There would be no oppression or murder or war. Dignity of human beings would prevail. One would not have to suffer on their deathbeds, as wishes for dignity and (self) love would be respected. One would not have to be exposed to expanded periods of pain. One would not rob their neighbor or cause them harm. One would neither judge nor condemn. One would know the truth of eternal life. One would live in loving awareness.

The potential to alleviate vast suffering is available. The measures and solutions have been handed to you. Ease the complications and look within.

Each individual has the loving wisdom and guidance. Each person has the capacity to realize what is truly right and to contribute to the wellbeing of self and the other. Each individual has the capacity to assist in the alleviation of humanity's suffering.

Honor you and your loved ones in your home, and care for those at your doorstep. You are all part of humanity; humanity is you, the individual; you are humanity. Your individual contribution will change the world.

I sense your feelings of powerlessness at times, but feeling powerless is a farce. I'm using the metaphor of the stillness of a lake. Even though the analogy is not new, it explains the essence of the truth. If one was to take action and throw a pebble of love into the lake, the immediate impact would be observed, and such it is with the immediate impact of your actions. The larger the pebble, the bigger the impact. To continue the symbolism of throwing the pebble: following the immediate impact, the effect would ripple outward and outward, until it would reach the shores where a transference of energy would then occur. Some of the embankment could erode, causing a bush to receive more water, allowing its berries to grow. These berries will feed the bird. The seeds from the berries are dropped and grow into plants. A bee goes on to pollinate the flower of the plant, the flower grows the fruit... and on and on the effect and release of love and positive contribution goes, in support of creation. And such it is with your actions.

Through each positive contribution, through each act of kindness, through each positive thought, the level of awareness is being raised and the level of suffering is decreasing. The wellbeing of humanity rises. Part of the soul's spiritual growth on this earth is the understanding of this knowledge – how each positive contribution, large or small, is valid and crucial in its effect on the ripple of life.

We are aware that many of you may feel disillusioned with your contributions, as it appears that poverty and suffering have only increased within your earthly conditions. Please be aware however, the global state of unconditional love and care has the potential to increase vastly, and now is the time to bring along the chance and raise the awareness amongst all.

Through your visual devices, the impact of the worldwide suffering may have been witnessed and felt on a larger scale, but through this shared experience (of the suffering), the acts of kindness and care have slowly started to expand. The visual experience of the suffering through the devices assists in attaining a deeper understanding of the suffering, which now has the capacity to catapult many individuals into loving action. And we honor you for that.

I know you are struggling with the notion that some organizations and institutions created to assist your disadvantaged and poor, could be working mainly to the benefit of themselves. Again, there is some truth in this in certain cases, and as discussed earlier on, those responsible for deceiving others for the benefit of self will experience expansive soul suffering, regret and an eternal longing to redeem themselves. Simultaneously, each act of true giving and of true support contributes to the overall wellbeing of humanity and brings it closer to the Divine state of knowledge and consciousness. As more individuals throw their loving pebbles, the ripple effect is grander and of greater result, reaching the shores and affecting humanity expansively and beyond.

As stated before, there are those who act out of greed for themselves. Simultaneously though, there are those who have diverted from the selfish path of increasing their power, and have dedicated their lives to helping others and giving vast amounts of wealth back in favor of the overall wellbeing of humanity. These individuals are embraced, just as the poor child is embraced for her acts of kindness. Acting selflessly is never truly selfless, since the true reward lies in the gift of giving and its unique contribution to the wellbeing of humanity and its decrease in suffering.

Becoming aware of the need to raise the level of vibration in each moment of one's life forms a large part of the true purpose of the incarnation on earth. Any contribution or act of love and kindness is an act towards the soul of self, as much as to the soul of the other. Any act that contributes to the decrease of suffering is one of great purpose, importance and soul reward. Any one of you who is struggling with the concept of meaning within your earthly existence will find the answer through giving love to self and others, and through contributing to the wellbeing of humanity at large. The intention of giving, the choosing of love, is where the meaning lies. In choosing love over hate, one raises the level of awareness. The question of "What would love do?"

should always be posed and in doing so, the answer will be received.

WHAT WOULD LOVE DO?

Extending the hand of love can often occur through small, yet significant actions. Each and every moment in life invites one to act from either love or anger and fear. The realization that each small moment and your response to it is of great significance, is a crucial realization in your path of spiritual growth and understanding. This knowledge applies to the response to oneself as much as the response to the other, since self and the other are essentially one.

The capacity to choose love and acknowledgment of Divine Self is, in fact, the choice for love of other (and all) simultaneously. Honoring the inner Divine creation and wellbeing of self is directly related to honoring the Divine creation and wellbeing of the other.

Dismissing violence towards self and alleviating suffering of self subsequently increases the capacity to love oneself and therefore the other. It is of great importance that you stop the torture of self immediately, that you stop the negative self-judgment and self-sabotage. It's important to stop the shame, forever.

The time is now to embrace the beautiful Divine creature you are, accept that you are deserving of receiving love, and embrace your capacity to give love. Only when self is healed and respected can a true understanding of the Divine connection be understood, then the path to healing all others will be opened up.

Every simple act of love, towards oneself as much as the other, is one in line with the Divine and therefore in line with your true essence. Following the principles of kindness, compassion, non-judgment, patience and love will pave the way to a healing of all – of you, the all-loving soul, of humanity and the precious earth you inhabit. Each act in line with the true essence of who you are is one of grandeur, grace and soul fulfillment.

In moments when one's anger rises, the question of "What would love do?" should be posed. Since your perceived opponent is also part of the Divine, and often reflects some of your own personality traits, the question of "What would love do?" is helpful towards self as much as the other. In your current times, you have frequent occurrences of rage when (literally) traveling on your highway of life. Actions involving oversight or simple mistakes are easily met by instant condemnation and aggressive responses without a true understanding as to why the mistake was made, or what the perceived offender could be going through. They may be in dire straits and their mistakes most probably have nothing to do with you.

Catching the mistakes of others in a safety net of understanding and forgiveness gives the other the opportunity to react with love, rather than anger, therefore expanding the collectiveness of love.

If, in contrast, one lets themselves be aggravated by the actions of the unexpected other, the simple phrase of "What would love do?" should provide the answer. One will remember to be compassionate and kind, and act with forgiveness towards the other, rather than react with judgment or enraged aggravation. This will provide the other with the opportunity to correct themselves, which is not only desirable for the other but also for the self, as it provides instant peace and a sense of acting in the right way.

On a bigger scale, the same applies. As nemesis and self are part of one, the one who saves the enemy in battle is the one who understands the truth and the one who lowers their weapon is the one who stands up for what is right. The enemy is a creation of your shared ego-understanding, rather than the alignment of your shared Divine Consciousness. The enemy concept, as created by the (shared) ego-understanding, has taken its own direction away from the path of truth. As the concept of the enemy is based on negative thought patterns, a simple change of perception, attitude and action can change a volatile situation to one of kindness and peace. If two of your most aggressive and volatile world leaders were to be dropped off on a rugged mountain top with only each other to rely on while making their way down, they would be friends by the time they reached the valley.

In shaking the hand of your nemesis and sharing a meal, the Divine connectedness will be revealed. In looking down the barrel of one's weapon and observing the eyes of the perceived enemy, one is looking into the eyes of the desperate self. As you are all one, saving your enemy is saving yourself. Choosing love over hate, kindness over malice, gratitude over resentment, each and every moment of your incarnated lives will bring you closer to the truth.

The truth of gratitude and loving existence. The truth of peaceful manifestation, of laughter, joy and fulfillment. The truth of peace and happiness for all. As humanity was intended, and as you all deserve.

Requesting Divine help, support or interference will always be heard. Raising the question of "What would love do?" will be answered, through the Divine voice and wisdom from within. Close attention to the support being offered needs to be paid. Opportunities to move towards a more desirable situation need to be taken and embraced. Acting in line with the Divine raises the vibrational level of awareness and supports the highest level of good of all involved. As one acts in line with this truth, one will be able to face their conscience without guilt or soul regret. It sets one free to move into the higher levels of vibration and evolve spiritually into the greater understanding of life.

SHARING WITH THE EARTH AND THE TRIBE

Spiritual practices and Divine connectedness have been part of ample cultures throughout the progression of your time. Your ancestors honored the spirits of the land and the angelic realms. They utilized their sixth sense, their inner voice, in their day-to-day lives. Decisions were preceded by quiet contemplation and meditation, and judgment was made with the help of solemn dialogue with the inner world and the resulting sense of knowing.

"Yes," I can hear you say, "but one doesn't build factories or roads based on a sense of knowing. Facts are needed." Please note that this is partly true. One needs facts and figures in your modern times. However, they need to serve and enhance the knowing that is already present, deep within. They need to support what one knows to be true, before certain directions are to be taken by humanity. In other words, the way in which you have expanded your material world has not been in line with what you know to be true, with what you know to be right:

The wellbeing of the planet, the wellbeing of humanity, of looking after one another as one would look after oneself, of sharing all resources and protecting all Divine creations of the earth, large and small.

The era has arrived in which an urgent shift is required. Even though many of your leaders strive for greater power based on the exploitation of people and resources, some are also well aware that the need for new social approaches and sustainable technologies is a must in order for humanity to thrive and survive.

The use and abuse of carbon-based resources will be catastrophic if immediate change is not pursued and environmentally friendly solutions applied. You have been supplied with renewable energies aplenty. Your sun and wind could sustain all demands for resources, and some of your leaders are doing the right thing in that they sacrifice their own wealth for the benefit of discovering better solutions and more sustainable ways of thinking. In your words: "They are the true heroes of your time."

What the leaders of the old approach need to remember is that the state of their own financial affairs is not going to provide them with a sense of achievement or happiness at the end of their lives. Rather, as they progress along the path of life, their own conscience will not stop questioning their choices in supporting the maltreatment of people, the destruction of nature, and eventually the demise of humankind. A sense of missed opportunities and loss of purpose will become overwhelming soul regrets if the demise of the earth has been supported by them. A one-hundred-and-eighty-degree turn in their way of thinking is required in order for their souls not to suffer. There is no greater soul reward than to contribute to a better humanity and a sustainable life, where all species can flourish and humanity's supplied gifts of creation are being honored and cared for.

The ongoing eradication of the supplied gifts of creation during the last century has devastated the angelic realm. The devastating acts of destruction by some individuals, based on power and greed while preaching the word of 'God', has not gone unnoticed.

As mentioned before, facing one's conscience in the presence of the great Creator, while having been responsible for the destruction of Divine gifts, leaves one deeply saddened and filled with profound shame and regret. Therefore, if at any moment in one's physical life, one becomes truly aware of his or her own actions of greed and destruction, one can still redirect the choices of their future being-ness and change the direction of their actions. By choosing to act in line with the Divine, one can still exponentially contribute to the wellbeing of humanity and change to a life of purpose, while also redeeming oneself in the eye of one's conscience. Simultaneously, every act of honoring and serving the creations of the Divine will affect the wellbeing of humanity in that it carries forward and raises the levels of vibration of human consciousness exponentially.

The simple willingness of a few could set the true wheels of change in motion in that a new economy can be created. Your governments and some of your supremely wealthy are required to prioritize urgently the financial and physical support of new sustainable technologies and enterprises. These investments, in line with the Divine purpose of each and every one of you, will create opportunities for a new and advanced workforce contributing to a higher vibrational standard of living and a betterment of humanity at large. Your recycling industry will grow and provide new living opportunities for many. Technologies utilizing renewable resources will lead your new sustainable economy, and a worldwide clean-up of your pollutants such as plastics and poisonous materials will follow suit. The level of vibrational energy will rise dramatically – bringing much greater joy, health and happiness for humanity at large.

A NEW SUSTAINABLE WORLD ORDER

In order to heal the earth and increase the happiness of humanity, a new sustainable world order is to be created. Do not fear as your economy will still thrive, but differently. You will still need homes, and modes of transport, and jobs. Yet the focus will be different. The focus will be on creating organically, with renewable and clean resources and with the overall wellbeing of humanity in mind. The new world order will support humanity, as much as the health of the planet. It will acknowledge the necessity of a clean environment, and respect the Divine gifts of nature, so it can benefit all.

The new sustainable world order will put economic growth in line with the virtues of the Divine Consciousness. Humanity and its wellbeing will feature first. Please realize that this is not a new notion. Much of your economic drive is already pushed by the desires of many for a happier and healthier life, in areas such as your food and tourist industries, your medical fields, your education, your hospitality industries, and your entertainment industries, which have grown considerably. Within the new sustainable world order, the elements of joyful creation, as well as serving others and nurturing the environment, will be added to the composition.

The economic value will change in that serving humanity will be considered the economy's real purpose, its real value. A monetary value will be attached to each and every action that will contribute to the happiness of every individual and to the good of all. Every choice, every investment will need to be examined with the same question in mind: how does this serve and benefit the greater good of all... how will this preserve our planet and its resources? The new sustainable world order will involve renewable energies, renewable jobs, renewable profits, renewable technologies, renewable production, renewable growth, renewable clean-ups, as well as recycling and re-use of goods.

These are urgent times. The fragility of humanity can't be denied. You are an intelligent and therefore strong species, but discounting the current malaise of your planet and the distress of your natural environment will contribute to humanity's fast demise. Those amongst you in powerful positions who simply ignore or dismiss the telling facts need to reconsider their personal responsibility towards future generations, and earnestly examine their conscience with regards to their decisions and the consequences on an individual soul level.

As stated before, the tremendous soul regret one experiences when knowingly opposing choices for the betterment of humanity can be deeply wounding and eternally hurtful. No choice will leave the growth of your souls untouched, and making the right choices in line with the greater good of all raises your level of consciousness into the spheres of the Divine.

Investments in renewable resources and technologies will need to be greatly increased. Leaders from countries with economies that currently rely on the exploitation of carbon-based resources and products will need to support and embrace the new sustainable paradigm. Their focus will need to shift to the development of renewable technologies, which will create a whole new and purposeful industry. The need for an awareness to speed up the renewable process is of great importance, and pressures from diverse world leaders will need to be applied.

Once the undoubted importance of the economic value in a new sustainable world order is recognized, many of your wealthy will shift their targets to include the wellness of the planet and all of humanity. Powerful individuals need to step away from personal gain and make decisions based on

Divine intent, as it will build their true legacy. It will provide them with eternal soul reward and turn them into the true heroes of your time. Any choice and action towards the betterment of humanity and in line with the Divine will be supported and embraced, and economic rewards will be realized.

The cost of pollution needs to be incorporated within the day-to-day responsibilities of the modern lifestyle, and each individual needs to take responsibility for each amount, large or small, as created by the individual. There is a colossal human and environmental price attached to creating waste, and the concern for waste disposal cannot be left in the hands of a few. Rather, each individual needs to consider the polluting effect of their purchase and conscientiously know their full responsibility for adding more trash onto the large amounts of waste. Each individual needs to take responsibility.

Every purchase, large or small, needs to be considered in its effects on the stockpile of waste and the sad reality that each acquisition needs to eventually end up somewhere. A strong urge for complete recycling and upcycling is made. As stated before, the responsibility can't be passed onto a few, as the problem is too large, and current waste solutions are not effective. The pile of daily waste is far too large for only a few to deal with.

Even though they are made to look adequate, the processing measures of refuse are a worldwide farce, and your lands and oceans are being suffocated and contaminated due to the enormous amounts of toxic and imperishable waste. When one views the vast amounts of rubbish as created within your consumption-driven societies, one needs to realize that the worldwide stockpile of lethal and enduring waste is asphyxiating you. One needs to ask oneself, "Will we let our babies sleep in a toxic pile of materials? Will we feed them contaminated product from the oceans and lands"?

There will be a moment when there is no turning back and this moment is at your doorsteps. The sadness as experienced within the angelic realm is vast and deep. The worldwide pollution is killing humanity and the native world. Worldwide action is now more urgent than ever. New research and commitment into biodegradable materials and new approaches as to reducing the production of plastics and synthetic materials, needs to be a prime commitment of every country and every government, no matter at what cost. You will need to make sacrifices and commitments, as individuals and governments, into cutting out waste. The voice of the Divine needs to be heard and followed as it will show the way and humanity will be rewarded.

On an individual level, the deep realization needs to set in that you are all good enough. There's no need to impress at the expense of your planet and its Divine gifts. How much of your purchased items end up polluting your soils or oceans? How much of your toxins end up destroying the atmosphere, contaminating the very air that you breathe? Practice daily gratitude for the Divine gifts of life – the gifts that flow freely, the ones that provide joy without your effort. Observe them, experience the bliss, rejoice in the offerings, and take part in life constructively and lovingly.

A fear of a recession because of the new sustainable economic order is ungrounded. Economies work when people believe that what they consume will expand their livelihoods. A belief in the importance of sustainable life lies at the core of the new economic force. A shift in global consciousness will occur whereby the true economic value of sustainable industries and products is acknowledged. The notion that the boundless overload of damaging consumer products and vast consumption at the current rate is good for your economies is a dangerous and outdated perspective. This belief erodes the purpose of your souls as well as the Divine intents, and it undermines humanity's happiness. The new sustainable economic way of thinking emphasizes the importance of human consumption that respects the Divine creation, and is in line with humanity's shared wellbeing and the joy and happiness of all, including the health and wellbeing of your planet and its glorious flora and fauna.

The production and consumption of goods that contribute to a healthier planet and a cleaner living environment will increase the true fulfillment and care for all. A blissful inner happiness will follow each sustainable choice one makes, as each choice adds to a grander, healthier and happier life for all. The reward of creating new technologies and goods that are in line with our soul's purpose and which contribute to a better living environment creates a new dimension to one's happiness. It connects each individual to the shared consciousness and aligns humanity with its Divine purpose.

As stated earlier, one will still drive their cars and operate machinery – just cleaner ones. One will still buy products – just more sustainable ones. Humanity will still advance technologically – just with a sustainable emphasis. Clean industries will be the new force driving your economies.

Your consumption will shift from a passive consumption focused on purchasing uninspiring and often harmful items, to a more active consumption whereby activity and leisure-based goods and services will prevail. Consumption of experiences will be the new economic force. Just as your music industries have developed into experience-based events, so will your activity-based leisure industries develop. Activities that inspire as well as bring people together will grow exceedingly and enhance the sense of shared happiness and joy.

Just as your computer-based technologies provided a new economic shift in your last decades, so will the new sustainable new order create new jobs, industries, activities and technologies.

Soul and inner fulfillment will be the main drive behind this new economic force. A renewed celebration of the arts and culinary experiences will also prevail. Small-scale production and consumption will be revered and a new esteem for traditional cultures, their ceremonies, knowledge, customs and practices, will ensue. Indigenous cultures will easily realign with a new shared purpose in that they will educate a large part of humanity through providing cultural knowledge and skills, based on their shared wisdom of traditional living. Building and crafting, as well as design and creative industries, will also flourish.

The time has arrived where livelihoods will only increase through sustainable demands as your current economic model is about to diminish the need for much human activity or individual contributions. The risks of increased technology and automation beyond the current point place you in danger of having your soul's earthly intent completely eroded – an intent which involves creativity, manifestation and contributing to humanity's wellbeing. The lack of human contributions in securing the necessities of life not only decreases the sense of soul purpose, but also leave the complete human spirit is disarray.

"Build and they will come" applies to a deep-seated acknowledgement that humanity is in desperate need of a new economic model that puts soul fulfillment and shared happiness at the core of its belief. The value that humanity puts towards a prosperous living environment will form the basis of the new sustainable economic world order, and it's up to each and every individual to face their own conscience and start making changes now – changes in line with the Shared Divine Consciousness, which increase humanity's happiness and benefit the quality of life experiences of all. Trust the new model, and a grand future will lie ahead.

CHILDREN'S CONNECTION TO THE DIVINE AND THEIR SOULS' PURPOSE

Children are your future, and the need for children to realize who they are is of crucial importance.

First of all, children need love and support, and the biggest support in the early stages of their young lives is you – father, mother, uncle, aunt or loving relative or friend. Being present, embracing them with your love and care, and carrying them through their early manifestation of life, teaching them the skills of life, are part of your Divine purpose. There is no greater gift than giving your child the unconditional love and attention she needs.

Abandoning your child is abandoning yourself and the unique creation you are, for the joy and soul reward lies in the nurturing of your children and the support of humanity's future. Children need your time and guidance, your attention, love and support. Children need to be supported in finding the exceptional guidance and wisdom from within. They need to be supported in how to recognize it and how to connect to it. They need to be encouraged to imagine and play, to create and feel joy, within the safety net of their parental support.

Imagination is a crucial factor in children's play. The ability to dream and imagine always precedes the ability to create, and as such the capacity to tap into the imaginary is of great importance in the preparation of life's challenges. Having a healthy imagination helps the child conceive of great ideas and come up with creative solutions to sometimes difficult problems. Just as your brilliant scientists and artists received support from the Divine, children, in connecting to the imaginary, will tap into the shared source of creativity and potential.

They will discover their true sense of self, their capacity to create, and feel that they are being supported when facing difficulties.

Currently, it has been observed that, unfortunately, curiosity and a natural urge to imagine and play are often set aside in favor of technological entertainment and ego-enhancing actions. They often encourage unhealthy competition and body appearances, as well as exterior polishes and grand possessions. The lack of connection to the inner compass erodes the child's capacity to distinguish right from wrong, as well as the capacity to recognize their unique strengths and qualities and the direction of their path through life. Play and imagination urgently need to be reinstated.

Imagination allows the child to align with their sense of purpose early in life and celebrate their unique qualities and desires. It also raises the awareness of the imprint of their soul. By taking away their ability to imagine, to play, and to create, and replacing it with a level of technological or passive entertainment, the child feels disconnected from its source, and the risk of wander and being lost can easily occur later in life. Your statistics on drug and alcohol abuse, as well as self-harm, are of great concern. The high level of youth suicide is directly related to the loss of connection and a lack of purpose.

The child's awareness of their particular set of qualities and soul-driven desires help him on his path to discovering his unique purpose in life and the exclusive contribution to humanity. If these traits and desires go unrecognized by the child herself, and the soul path remains unclear, the young adult literally becomes lost and confused. Instead, the outer world imposes consumption-based ideas and desires onto the child, as well as ego-based activities which distract from the Divine path as mapped out in the footprint of the child's life.

The fragile polish of the ego's exterior is no match for a strong inner connection to the Divine, and your children are in desperate need of realigning with whom they truly are. The child needs time and space to recognize their unique affinities and burning soul desires, which shape the foundation of their path in life. Imaginative play and contemplative time in nature are therefore of crucial importance in the child's life. The connection to the soul's purpose is always directly related to a sense of joy, and for the child it is imperative that passion is discovered through imaginative play and creation. Part of the soul's purpose always involves creation of ideas and actualization of inner dreams and desires.

If the child is not assisted in tuning into the whispers from within and recognizing their calling and unique desires, a depressive state can easily occur later in life. From a very young age, the child should be aware of their inner guidance and unconditional Divine support, so that at any moment in their life they can call upon the wisdom from within, especially when faced with moral dilemmas and choices between right and wrong. Teaching children the practice of daily meditation, and recognizing the guiding voice from within, is of great importance.

It is crucial that education also involves creative and contemplative subjects, so the child stays connected to the Shared Consciousness during their academic development. Incorporating and developing the notion of gratitude and compassion in their daily learning and practice is of utmost importance, as well as an understanding of sustainable practices and preservation of resources and life. Music, dance, creative arts and the development of life skills, as well as imaginative problem solving, should also be a large part of the curriculum. The study of nature and biology and the practice of joyful sport should be incorporated as well. Science and language should be encouraged through practical application in the earlier years so that a sense of relating can develop. This, in turn, will develop and stimulate the academic desires for deeper levels of understanding and concepts of greater intricacy and complexity. The desire to learn will originate from within the individual, rather than be forced upon them.

THE TENDERNESS OF ALL

The peace, the tranquility, the purity of your souls, the tenderness of all. The memory of this is embedded in your being.

To return to this consciousness is attainable during your earthly existence and the Source of all is right here, with you. The practice of reconnection to the inner Divine will lead you to the remembrance of who you are. It will enhance your daily earthly lives. The simplicity of being, the tenderness of all that has been given, needs to be observed and embraced. For true peace, true happiness and joy is attainable at any moment in your lives. Observe, take in, embrace. Do not let concerns, worries or pain distract you from the return to all that is. It wants to encourage you to realign. To give you hope and strength in moments of despair, of deep sadness and pain. The angelic realm will hear you, support you and enhance your state of being. It will help you grow and see, and find new hope and opportunities.

It will help you find joy, purpose, happiness and peace.

One must not forget that all is provided for, all is taken care of, especially when help is needed. Go within and formulate your desires in line with the love and kindness of the Divine, and your call will be heard. Your needs will be met. External authority won't provide the answer, but your inner guidance and connection will. Call upon the support and listen to the quiet voice within. Do not hasten but let the answer appear in perfect timing.

Life is to be taken step by step and one cannot hasten the progression of life. Each delicate step needs to be considered and taken with love and joy, rather than with greed, judgment, or condemnation. Your fellow human beings face their own obstacles, and from your limited perception all cannot be observed or understood. Trust the direction from within and rather than judge, compassion needs to be applied. Simultaneously, one cannot underestimate the compassion for self, as that too, is of utmost importance in finding peace and guidance.

We observe so much hatred and dislike of self, when your essence is bathed in our love, as you are our heavenly creation.

The urgency of giving up self-hate and allowing our love, while sitting in silence, is once again emphasized. As you naturally, and without any hesitation or doubt, embrace your newborns with unconditional and pure love, so should you not hesitate to receive the unconditional love for you from the Divine. You are never alone. You are always supported. No matter who you are, no matter what you have done, you are unconditionally loved and you will always be forgiven if forgiveness is required by you.

The essence of your soul strives for alignment with the Divine and it is never too late to make changes in behavior and ask for forgiveness if one has not been in alignment with it. It is your very own conscience that is one's authority and causes you pain when the right actions have not been taken – that what one has done to others has always been done to self, and will be felt and examined when

159

facing one's own conscience when leaving your earthly existence. The pain experienced as done to others, in that very moment, is of far greater depth and magnitude than it was in your earthly life. It is this pain that has the capacity to overwhelm one with deep regret and desire for redemption.

The opportunities of redeeming oneself are therefor never to be underestimated. It is never too late to make amends and change one's course in life. Each and every one of you deserves love from self and others, and giving love and extending the hand of kindness is the greatest of soul rewards – in accordance with one's unique purpose of serving humanity and contributing to the wellbeing of all. As discussed earlier, the simple gestures of love can make a big difference in the lives of your fellow human beings and uplift the human experience of all.

In connecting to the wisdom from within, you will be directed in how to live in harmony with your loving essence, the source of who you truly are. You will sense how to express yourself in perfect alignment with the Divine. You will know how to create and be creative, and contribute to the wellbeing of self as well as others. To share stories with your tribe and be mesmerized by the gentle flames of the fire of life.

You will be directed to spend more time with others, to simply laugh and dance, and most of all to feel joy... whether surrounded by family, or your children, or friends. Being face to face with other human beings is still a big part of the main purpose of your lives. Again, if God intended you to always communicate via a device, He wouldn't have given you a body. The physical experience of your human incarnation is of utmost importance and the goal of fulfilling your purpose is the most extraordinary reason for partaking in the dance of life.

As you live in harmony with your loving essence, you are invited to observe all that is giving around you: the sky, the forests, the lakes, the oceans and all other heavenly creatures of joy, such as the flowers and the birds. Observe and absorb them as if your life depends on it. Because the reality is that it does (depend on it).

You have been given the beautiful landscapes, and mountains and lakes, and fields of abundance. You have been given the sun to warm you and the wind, which moves your air aplenty. You have rain and snow and skills to gather and sow and reap. You have been given your fellow human beings to interact with and with whom to share joy. You have been given the vast consciousness of the Divine to tap into and from which to create. With our guidance, with our support.

You have the power to make changes – changes to be together, to run in the fields, to play and create music and beauty, and to be aware of your beautiful children. It's your birthright to feel real joy. It's your birthright to be happy. Extend the hand of love and tap into the joy within.

My message is one of Shared Divine Love, of a Divine state of being where one can trust and live in joy and peace: within and 'without' (outward). Trust self, the other, and find the truth within. Look around and share the love, with each choice coming your way.

Expand your love to your family, to your neighbor, to your nemesis and to your friend. Expand your love to all that has been given: the earth, its resources, its flora and its fauna, and save all. Through your love, through our love. Through the love of the Divine Consciousness, which constitutes *all that is*.

ACKNOWLEDGMENTS

My deep gratitude goes out to my loving and always supportive husband, for his unconditional love, joy and support. You are an absolute gem; I could not have written this book without you. I am also very grateful for the support of my wonderful copyeditor Vicki Englund, for all your expertise, eye for detail and your professional and analytical feedback. You always have my back. Your contribution has been vitally important. I thank you with all my heart. To my creative and loving son Cairo, I want to extend a big thank you for your beautiful photography, your patience and your support in putting the cover of this book together. You are a real talent and it was an absolute joy to work and laugh with you. Lastly I want to thank my friends from 'Your Year of Miracles', for helping me hold the intention; Marci and Debra for your wonderful leadership, and Wendy, Rosie, Martina, Vera, and Michelle for all your love and support.

NOTES

www.ingramcontent.com/pod-product-compliance
Lightning Source LLC
Chambersburg PA
CBHW051827040426
42447CB00006B/412